COURTROOM SURVIVAL

THE OFFICER'S GUIDE TO BETTER TESTIMONY

DEVALLIS RUTLEDGE

COPPERHOUSE PUBLISHING COMPANY

1590 Lotus Road
Placerville, California 95667
(916) 626-1260

Your Partner in Education
with
"QUALITY BOOKS AT FAIR PRICES"

COURTROOM SURVIVAL
THE OFFICER'S GUIDE TO BETTER TESTIMONY

Developmental Editor - Derald Hunt

Library of Congress Catalog Number 87-70528
ISBN 0-942728-15-7 Paper Text Edition

Printed in the United States of America.

COURTROOM SURVIVAL

*The Officer's Guide
To Better Testimony*

CONTENTS

Do you ever look through the table of contents to get some idea of what's inside a book, to see if you might want to read it? And then you find a table of contents with a list of chapter titles like "Nature and Scope," "Organization and Purpose," "Modification of Rule," and "Miscellaneous Applications." You can't tell much about a book from titles like that (except that it's probably boring as hell).

So I've made my list of contents a little bit more than just a "table." Each chapter title is followed by a summary of what that chapter is about. You can read this section in two minutes, and you'll get a good idea of whether there's anything of value to you in the book.

be something you maintain and keep current against the day you are called as an expert witness.

My final words to you about the proper relationship between cops and prosecutors, and how each can contribute to better courtroom performance and more convictions.

All of the examples I use in the book are taken from actual trials and hearings, and from my personal experience. I've changed some names and addresses.

None of the suggested responses that I show are meant for you to memorize and repeat verbatim in your next testimony. They are simply <u>models</u> to demonstrate the proper techniques and approaches that I discuss.

This book is written in an informal, person-to-person manner, with an abundance of contractions and a liberal use of the pronouns "I" and "you," for one simple reason: I want it to be <u>easy</u> for you to read and use. Telling you not to chew gum in the courtroom is not *training*—it's just an *insult*. What's inside this book is practical information that every officer needs; I hope you'll take time to arm yourself with it before your next court appearance.

WHY READ THIS BOOK?

Cops are fearless. You trade lead with robbers and killers and barricaded kooks. You drive street cars in 120 mph pursuits. You put on an old t-shirt, grow a beard (men only), and plant yourself in the middle of a dope ring where you're outnumbered 20 to 1. And even worse, you wade in between a feuding husband and wife who are mad enough at each other to kill you.

You tolerate these daily dangers reasonably well, because you're well-trained, well-armed, well-equipped, and well-suited to the job. Your experience gives you confidence in your ability to control the situation. So when you spot the trouble up ahead, or get dispatched to handle the dangerous call, you don't freeze up and break out in a sweat—you set your mind and body for the action, and you handle it with all the skill and courage of a combat commander. Emergency after emergency, you're steady as a rock.

What does it take to make you shake? If you're like I was when I was a cop, it's something not nearly as dangerous as a gunfight, not nearly as fast-paced as a pursuit, not nearly as intricate as an undercover dope buy, and not nearly as explosive as a family disturbance. If you're like I was, you lose your comfortable self-confidence when you take your seat on the witness stand, with the eyes and ears of one judge, twelve jurors, two lawyers and a room full of spectators trained on *you.*

Suddenly, you're not the one in control of the situation. You're not calling the shots. This is the realm of the lawyers—the prosecutor and defense attorney—and now they're going to put *you* through the same kind of interrogation you're used to subjecting the *crooks* to.

Sure, the *defendant* is the one whose guilt or innocence is on trial. But we all know that you are on trial, too—your credibility, your professionalism, your knowledge, your competence, your judgment, your conduct in the field, your use of force, your adherence to official policies, your observance of the defendant's rights—they're all on trial. Suddenly, you'd like to trade the safe, clean, calm courtroom for the dirtiest street in town!

When your testimony begins, you may start off fairly cool and collected. And maybe by the time you finish direct examination, you get the feeling you're going to survive. But by the time a competent defense attorney is through working you over with a gruelling cross-examination, you're about ready to run over and hug him for the merciful relief of those longed-for words: "No further questions."

I know the feeling. I know what it's like to sit on the stand hour after hour and contend with a hair-splitting, nit-picking attorney. I know how insulted and resentful you feel when it seems like you're having to defend yourself for just doing a good job of arresting criminals. I remember how frustrating it is to be trying to tell what happened, only to be interrupted with an endless stream of objections, and a judge sternly warning you to "just answer the questions," and telling the jury to disregard your last response.

And as a prosecutor, I know what it's like to sit helplessly by while the defense attorney makes you look like a confused, incompetent, bungling rookie. I see that plea in your eyes when you look to me as if to say: "Help me! Do something! Get me out of this mess!"

But there's usually nothing I can do. I can't stand up in front of the jury and say: "Let's excuse the officer, your honor—I think he's had enough." I can't interrupt the trial and tell you how to testify. I can't pass you notes and tell you what you're doing wrong. And I can't start using a lot of unnecessary objections to give you a breather, unless I want the jury to realize that I'm just trying to rescue a sinking witness.

If I could stop the action when you step down off the stand—if I could get you when you've just gone through an uncomfortable cross-examination, and set you down, and talk to you for an hour or two about

All kinds of emergencies are all in a day's work . . .

. . . so is testifying.

how to be a better witness—I'd have your attention; I know you'd listen.

I can't do that. No prosecutor can. But there's something even better. If I can get you to spend the time it takes to read this book, you ought never have to go through an uncomfortable cross-examination again. And you ought to become as confident and as proficient on the witness stand as you are in the field.

You don't have too many choices. If you're going to wear a badge, you're going to be called as a witness. You can't make it go away. Some cops try, I know. They call up and hint to the prosecutor that a plea bargain would be alright with them. They go on vacation. They call in sick. They lose their subpenas. And they complain loudly that all the time they waste testifying in court keeps them from getting any police work done.

But testifying *is* police work. It's the final phase of a police officer's work on a case. If the cop isn't a good witness—if his testimony isn't accurate and convincing— all the rest of his police work is just a futile exercise. No matter how brilliant the investigation, how careful the arrest, and how thorough the report, if an officer isn't just as competent on the stand as he is in the field, he's just processing bodies.

There's no point in making *arrests* if we aren't going to get *convictions*. Your share of the responsibility for seeing to it that your arrestees get convicted doesn't end when you lock up the body and book the evidence. You're only doing half the job unless you follow through with a useful report and credible testimony. (If you haven't done so, I recommend you read my book, *THE NEW POLICE REPORT MANUAL,* on the easy way to write better reports.)

Testifying in court is part of your job. If you've never liked that part of being a police officer, or if you've often felt that it was your weakest attribute, the answer isn't to find new ways to avoid testifying. The answer is to find new ways to gain the same kind of skill and confidence on the witness stand that you have in the field. Then, hopefully, you'll be as comfortable in the courtroom as you are on the streets, and you'll be as good at *convicting* the crooks as you are at *catching* them.

Our Southern California teletype once printed out an emergency weather bulletin after a Mexican earthquake. It warned of an imminent tsunami (a great sea wave caused by submarine earth movement or volcanic eruption). The bulletin cautioned that such waves may be up to 100 feet high, and move at tremendous speeds. In advising precautionary evacuation from coastal areas, the bulletin warned: *"Do not wait until you see the tsunami wave. By the time you see it, it will be too late."*

If you've never been through an unmerciful cross-examination on a case where you were ill-prepared to testify, don't wait until it happens before you find out how you could have saved yourself a lot of embarrassment, and maybe a conviction. By the time you get serious about being a better witness, it may be too late.

Now, I'm not going to try to kid you. Just reading this book isn't going to make you a seasoned expert. No book on any subject can do that. You also need *practice* at putting what you've learned into action. You can't get that practice anyplace but in court. There's no such thing as a book that can substitute for practical experience.

On the other hand, no amount of practical experience can compensate for shoddy preparation, incomplete understanding of your role as witness, and inept performance by an officer whose obvious uneasiness on the stand translates into low credibility with the jury—which translates into hung juries and acquittals.

I've seen traffic officers with many years of experience and hundreds of drunk-driving arrests to their credit get taken apart piece by piece on routine DUI arrests, sometimes by *good* defense attorneys, and sometimes by lawyers who were just barely *average*. And I couldn't count the times I've watched good felony cases crumble as effective cross-examination proved that even detectives and investigators with ten or fifteen years on the force can still be lousy witnesses.

Whether you've testified in hundreds of cases, or whether you're still dreading (or looking forward to) your first courtroom experience, you probably could benefit from the trial lawyer's point of view on police testimony. So I've collected suggestions from prosecutors and defense attorneys alike (as well as a few comments from trial judges). The information in this book is intended to give you a solid foundation for the practical experience that will make you a good witness.

Preparation, natural approach, understanding of defense tactics, and knowledge of how to handle them comfortably—these are the weapons of the well-armed police witness. Just as you wouldn't go into the alley on Saturday night without your guns and handcuffs, you shouldn't go into the criminal courtroom without the ammunition you need to lock the last door on the crook you've arrested.

When you take the stand, you're on trial. Your department is on trial. Often, the case will turn on *your credibility* with the jury. Don't blow it through your neglect to arm yourself adequately as a witness. Don't wait until you find yourself squirming on the witness stand in a crowded courtroom, with visions of a tsunami wave crashing on your head. No matter how much you already know (or think you know), take time for a little training. If you ever take the stand again, it'll pay off for you.

□

SET
YOURSELF
UP

If you really want to get an early start on an easy time at the witness stand, get into the habit of thinking ahead to the trial while you're still out in the field. Then carry through with that approach right up to the filing of your report.

A mistake some officers make (I was guilty of it, too) is in becoming arrest-oriented, and conviction-indifferent. When I was a rookie cop, running up and down the streets in a black-and-white and looking for action, I somehow got the mistaken idea that *my* job was to *arrest* criminals and that it was the *prosecutor's* job to *convict* them, if he could. I didn't realize how much the prosecutor depended on *me* to help him get the conviction.

And I didn't realize at first how much *my* actions in the field (and my written reports) *limited* the prosecutor in his job of convicting the people I arrested. I was pretty slow in learning that what I was giving the prosecutor when I presented my case to him was a plaster cast, with the issues, defenses, and limits of the case already defined and set by the things I had done, or failed to do.

The fact is that the police investigation and the report are the raw material of the prosecution. Unless your local prosecutor is a magician, he is not going to be able to work too many miracles with an incomplete case. And since *he's* thinking ahead to trial when he reviews your arrest, he may decide not to file a criminal complaint if you've made his job of prosecuting too tough. If you keep hearing your prosecutor complain that "You're not giving me anything to work with," it's time to ask yourself whether you're too arrest-oriented and conviction-indifferent.

From the moment you get involved in a case, you've got to be thinking ahead to a possible trial. You've got to be picturing yourself on the witness stand, describing your actions and observations in detail. The best way to do that is to continually ask yourself: "What if they ask me about this in court?" If you're continually framing your answers to this same question about every aspect of the case, you'll be ready when they finally *do* ask you in court.

Some cops have told me the reason they don't treat every case as if it's going to trial is because very few cases ever actually *get* that far. But there are two basic reasons why most cases never get to trial: they're either so *well-prepared* by the investigating officers that the defense agrees to a straight plea (or a stiff plea bargain), or they're so *poorly-prepared* by the investigating officers that the prosecution declines to file, or bargains them away for a reduced sentence.

If your cases are never going to trial because the *defense* doesn't want to try them, there's a good chance you're the kind of cop who prepares every case as if he expects it to be tried. On the other hand, if your cases are being bargained away by a conscientious *prosecutor,* you're probably not giving him a case that's ready to try. And if that's happening, you're probably not thinking ahead to trial as you investigate and report your cases.

If your cases are getting to trial (or at least to some kind of hearing), but you're getting worked over pretty badly by the defense lawyers, you're probably not setting yourself up right. You're probably leaving yourself open to damaging attacks because you're not asking yourself: "What if they ask me about this in court?"

Bear in mind that anything you *do* or *say* in the field may be played back to you in court. That means you've got to conduct yourself in the field at all times as if the judge and jury were right behind you, looking over your shoulder, and listening to everything you say. If you don't act accordingly, your own words can come back to haunt (and embarrass) you.

EXAMPLE

> Q: *(By defense attorney) What did you do next, Officer?*
> A: *I ordered them to halt.*
> Q: *Exactly what did you say?*
> A: *Well, . . . uh, I can't remember exactly.*
> Q: *Was it something like: "Freeze, motherfuckers, or I'll blow you a new asshole?"*
> A: *Uh . . . uh . . . I think it was . . . may have been something like that.*

* * *

> Q: *Did the defendants tell you that they would be glad to have their case decided in court?*
> A: *Yes, I believe they did.*
> Q: *And did you then say: "You pukes are going to find out how the system works, if you think you're going to kiss the judge's ass and stroke a bunch of jerk jurors on this thing?"*
> A: *Well, uh . . I may have said something similar to that at the time . . .*

This officer's credibility has just gone to zero with the middle-class jury and the judge. He said something in the field (or in the station) that he can't live with very comfortably at trial. He never would have done that if he had only acted as if judge and jury were looking on and listening in as he dealt with the crooks. He should have been repeating to himself: "What if they ask me about this in court?" He should have been setting himself up for an easy time on the stand. Instead, of course, he set himself up for a sting.

Now, sometimes you may <u>have</u> to talk rough to somebody, or else risk getting ignored or laughed out of the neighborhood. If you find that necessary (though there's usually a more clever way to handle it), you've got a couple of options that won't embarrass you at trial. Here's one:

EXAMPLE

> **Q**: *What did you do next, Officer?*
> **A**: *I ordered them to halt.*
> **Q**: *Exactly what did you say?*
> **A**: *I can't guarantee this is exact, but I believe I said: "Freeze, turkeys, or I'll shoot."*

Or, if your experience or force of habit seems to dictate harsher language, try to trick the defense attorney into giving you a chance to explain *why* you sometimes use "foul" language. Why do you have to *trick* someone before you can explain things? If you've ever testified before, you know that the rules of court severely restrict you in answering questions. If your answer goes beyond the scope of the question, you'll be interrupted and cut off and the jury will be instructed to disregard your "non-responsive" explanations.

Therefore, unless the attorney specifically *asks* you to explain something, you won't be allowed to do so. You'll only get to answer as much as the attorney calls for with his question. Then you're stuck like this:

EXAMPLE

> **Q**: *Was it something like: "Freeze, motherfuckers, or I'll blow you a new asshole?"*
>
> **A**: *Yes, but the <u>reason</u> I said that was . . .*
>
> **Q**: *Objection! Non-responsive.*
>
> **The Court**: *Everything after the word "yes" will be stricken. The jury will disregard it. Officer, just answer the questions.*

You see? You're sitting there with a good explanation you'd like to give as to why you talked that way, but unless the attorney asks you to explain, you won't get the chance. The jury will get an unfavorable impression of you that you and the prosecutor may not be able to dispel.

Now, no defense attorney in his right mind is ever going to give you a chance to explain anything. The dumbest question any attorney can ever ask an opposing witness is "why?" So, if you're ever going to get the chance to explain yourself before the jury's impression of you gets set in their heads, you've got to know how to *provoke* the defense attorney into giving you a chance to explain.

How do you do it? You use something I call an "unexpected qualifier." Instead of simply saying "yes" when he asks you if you used that dirty language, you qualify your answer with an unexpectedly provocative word or two that *challenges* the attorney to ask "why?"

If he thinks he's embarrassed you by repeating your dirty language to the jury, he might expect you to try to deny it, or to try to clean it up a little bit, or to sheepishly admit that you did use the quoted language. What he would *not* expect is that you would not only *admit* using the language, but would do so in such a way as to make it look like there was absolutely nothing to be embarrassed about. When you get him to take this bait, he's going to get greedy (and careless); he's going to think he's got you again—not only do you *use* dirty language, you come into court and act stupidly *proud* of it. Now he's going to reveal your stupid thinking to the jury. He's going to ask you *why* you answered the way you did:

EXAMPLE

Q: *Was it something like: "Freeze, motherfuckers, or I'll blow you a new asshole?"*

A: *Of course!*

Q: *What do you mean,   "Of course;" why did you say that?*

A: *I'm glad you asked me that. I said "Of course," because I've learned through experience in dealing with criminal suspects that most of them respond to rough language. If I give a command in mild language, they won't always take me seriously, and we wind up in a fight or a chase. Using street talk and even profanity is usually the only thing that gets through to the kind of people I have to deal with out there.*

"What if they ask me about this in court?"

See how the officer tricked the attorney into giving him a chance to explain his use of dirty language? Whenever you want to provoke the attorney into asking you *why* you did or didn't do something, use an unexpected qualifier to answer his "did-you-or-did-you-not" question. Some of these provokers are: definitely; certainly; certainly not; naturally; naturally not; not *then;* not *at first;* yes, *initially;* and one that always does the trick: "Yes, and no."

Better than being able to get your explanation *in* is not *having* to explain anything you've done or said. So when you say or do something in the field or station, you ought to be thinking ahead to whether you want to live with it if the defense attorney plays it back to the jury.

Set yourself up when you start working the case. In the middle of the trial, you can't go back and un<u>do</u> anything, or un<u>say</u> anything. So don't box yourself in with anything you can't live with in court.

Clear enough? Step number one to becoming a better witness is to grease your own way, right from the start. Set yourself up by thinking ahead to the trial, pretending judge and jury are always with you, and constantly asking and answering the question: "What if they ask me about this in court?"

□

BE PREPARED

You may never have thought of yourself as someone who takes much care in preparation. Most people like to think they're too experienced to have to worry much about preparing something that's just another part of their daily routine. But if you look closely, I bet you'll find that you do a lot more preparing than you realized.

Before you even got a job as a cop, you probably did everything you could to prepare for the exam and the oral interview. You talked to people who had been through it before to find out what kinds of questions you'd be asked. Maybe you went on a special diet-and-exercise routine to get ready for the physical. You shined your shoes and carefully selected your clothes for the oral board. All that *preparation* was just to get the job.

And once you were hired, there was orientation, the academy, and supervised OJT. You memorized the city map, the radio code, and the location of every donut and coffee shop in town. **Preparation.**

Even in your daily routines, look at all the preparing you do. When you get to the locker room, you deck yourself out in an imposing uniform and badge, you strap on a sidearm, you fill all the holders on your Sam Brown with batons, saps, chemical mace, ammo, handcuffs, flashlights, pack sets and whistles. All this battle gear is in **preparation** for your next eight-hour war on crime.

Then you go to roll call assembly for more **preparation**: your briefing on the current status of the campaign—which cars were stolen last night; which places were burglarized; who's wanted for murder; and which group of citizens are complaining that they're not seeing enough (or are seeing too many) police cars in their area.

Before you hit the street, you check out your unit— shotgun's loaded; flares, first-aid, and fire extinguisher are in the trunk; lights, siren and radio work; no dope or weapons are stashed under the back seat; there's gas in the tank, and your wristwatch is working. All prepared to roll.

But your preparation never stops. Before you make a carstop, you call it in, and you pick your spot up ahead. That's preparation. Before you go into a house after someone, you surround it with cops. Preparation. Enroute to the silent robbery alarm, you start thinking of all the possible escape routes, and you radio for units to block them. Preparation. Sergeant's exam coming up? Preparation.

See how it goes on and on? Nobody—not even the most street-wise narc or vice cop (we all know they're the coolest of all, don't we?)—crashes along like a malt liquor bull without thinking ahead and *preparing* for what he's up against.

EXCEPT WHEN IT'S TIME TO TESTIFY. Strangely, many cops who do a first-rate job of preparing themselves for every other phase of their police work don't even *try* to get ready for court. They take the stand in a nine-month old case without a moment's preparation, and clumsily proceed to help the defense attorney make a wreck of their good police work, and simultaneously lay the foundation for a lawsuit against themselves.

Preparation for court is just as necessary—and just as important—as preparation for any other aspect of police work. What's the point of risking your life in the field to get criminals arrested, if you're not going to bother doing everything you can reasonably do to avoid losing the case in court? Not much point at all, is there? So let's look into some easy ways to get yourself ready for court.

The first and most obvious thing you do after you get your subpena is to pull your report and see what the case is about. If you have a *serious* case (homicide, rape, kidnap, robbery, etc.), you may want to make yourself a **preparation checklist,** and check things off as you get them done. If possible, it's a good idea to talk to the prosecutor and see if there's anything in particular he wants you to concentrate on.

You're well-prepared to win in the field . . . make sure you're prepared to win in court, too.

For most *routine* cases, a checklist would be helpful, but not required. Your report, and the seriousness of the case, will tell you what preparatory steps are in order, and they will dictate the content of your checklist. Here are some things to consider.

☐ READ YOUR REPORT

You wouldn't believe how many veteran police officers get on the witness stand completely cold, on a case that may be anywhere from two months to two years old. In the meantime, they've made dozens of similar arrests. The specific details of *this* case are fused into the memory of any number of both newer and older cases, and yet the cop expects to get up on the witness stand and selectively pick out just the facts of this one case, without bothering to refresh his recollection from a report he wrote while everything was fresh in his mind.

That in itself is almost criminal. Look at it this way: every state, no matter where you live, has a statute making it illegal to assist or give aid and comfort to a criminal in order to help him escape conviction or punishment. If you get on the witness stand without knowing your report inside and out—the way the defense attorney knows it—your testimony is probably going to give considerable aid and comfort to the guy you arrested. You very well may turn the case his way, just enough to give a reluctant jury some excuse for a "reasonable doubt." Your testimony may be just the thing to help a guilty defendant escape conviction and punishment.

Do you think that's rare? Let me assure you, after my experience in hundreds of hearings and trials, that it's about as rare as commercials on TV. I'd like to sell a copy of this book for every time a juror has told me: "We thought the guy probably did it, but there were just too many discrepancies in the officer's testimony. He didn't seem to recall the case very well."

Unless your local prosecutor tells you that for some tactical reason he doesn't want you to review your report in a given case, you should *always* begin your preparation by reading your report. Whether it's a traffic citation or a murder arrest, don't get on the stand without reading what you've written. Don't do the crook any favors.

□ RE-READ YOUR REPORT

Before the defense attorney ever gets to trial, he's probably read your report ten times. As he listens to your testimony on direct, he's comparing everything you say on the stand with what you said in your report. And believe me, he'll catch every discrepancy, no matter how slight. Some of those discrepancies he'll use in cross-examination, to try to shake you up. Some of them he'll save for final argument, to point out to the jury that you put one thing in your report and said another thing on the stand. He'll argue that since you couldn't possibly have been right on both occasions, your credibility isn't worth relying on.

The only way to avoid giving the defense attorney this helping hand is to avoid testifying in conflict with your report. The only way to do *that* is to be sure that both your report and testimony are complete and accurate, and to know what's in your report—and what is not—before you raise your hand to be sworn in as a witness. At a minimum, you should read your report *twice* before continuing with your preparation, and at least *once more* the day of trial . . . or do you think it's okay for the *defense attorney* to know your report better than *you* do?

□ REVIEW PHOTOS AND TAPES

If these exist, pull them and look at or listen to them. I once had a commercial burglary trial where an important issue was whether or not some cartons of stolen parts had a distinctive green price sticker on them that would prove they came from the victim's business. The arresting officer testified that he was "certain" the cartons had <u>no</u> such stickers.

It was easy enough for me to prove that the cartons *did* have such stickers, because I had all of the cartons, as well as color photographs taken at the time of their recovery. In the photos, the priced side of the cartons were all facing the camera, and the green stickers stuck out like neon. Unfortunately, as soon as I introduced these photos and the cartons, the defense attorney had something to impeach the officer's credibility with:

Ladies and gentlemen, you'll recall how certain the officer was about the price stickers. We know now that he was absolutely wrong, don't we? And yet he told us he was <u>certain</u>! Now, how much credence can you place in the rest of his testimony?

If the officer had bothered to review the photos before trial, his testimony wouldn't have been wrong, and I wouldn't have wound up having to argue to the jury that they should still trust the remainder of his testimony, even though he obviously wasn't too reliable in part of it.

And it's even *more* embarrassing and damaging when you impeach yourself with your own voice. A cop who had tape recorded a burglar's confession got on the stand in a hearing on the voluntariness of the confession, and gave this testimony:

Q: *(By defense attorney) Officer, did you make any promises to the defendant in order to induce him to talk to you?*

A: *No, sir.*

Q: *You didn't promise to do any favors for him?*

A: *No, sir. In fact, I'm sure I probably told him that I <u>couldn't</u> make any promises.*

Q: *Did you discuss the subject of bail or release with him?*

A: *I don't believe the subject came up, as I recall.*

KNOW YOUR REPORT

If the defense attorney is more familiar with what is in your report than you are, he has you at a great disadvantage. And that's precisely where he wants you.

Don't do the defense any favors. Read your report enough times to be sure you know what you said—and what you didn't—before you get on the witness stand.

Q: *Then you're certain you never told him—before you started your questioning—you never told him anything about bail—never made a promise, that is, to do him any favors relative to bail in order to persuade him to discuss the charges with you?*

A: *That's correct.*

Q: *You tape recorded your interview with the defendant, didn't you, Officer?*

A: *Yes, sir.*

Q: *And this is a copy of that tape, just as everything happened—this is a copy that you've provided me with, is that right?*

A: *That's right.*

Q: *Now, Officer, let me play just a small—Your Honor, I would like to play just a small segment of this tape to refresh, or see if it refreshes the officer's recollection.*

The Court: *Very well. Go ahead. Do you have it up to the place where you want to play it?*

Attorney: *Yes, Your Honor.*

(Tape:) *Now, uh, Denny, I appreciate the fact that, uh, you've been very cooperative. And I just want to let you know that I think you're a good bet for an O.R. release—in fact, I'm going to see what I can do to get you an O.R., OK? How does that sound to you?*

Q: *Now, Officer, did you recognize that voice?*

A: *Yes, sir. That was myself.*

Q: *That was you, talking about the subject of whether the defendant was going to get out O.R. or on bail, wasn't it?*

A: *Yes, sir.*

Q: *And that was you, promising to see what you could do to get an O.R., wasn't it?*

A: *Yes.*

Q: *You don't do that for everyone you arrest, do you, Officer?*

A: *No.*

Q: *Then would you say it was more or less a favor that you were promising?*

A: *In that context, I guess you would say that.*

Q: *And you were doing it in return for what you called "being very cooperative," weren't you?*

A: *Well, in a—yes, more or less.*

Q: *Then when you testified earlier that you never made any promises, you were wrong, weren't you, Officer?*

A: *Well, I didn't remember exactly what I said.*

Q: *And when you testified you never discussed any favors, you were wrong, weren't you?*

A: *Yes.*

Q: *And when you testified the subject of bail never came up, you were wrong, weren't you?*

A: *Yes.*

Q: *And when you testified you never discussed bail or release, that was wrong too, wasn't it?*

A: *Yes.*

Q: *And was it after you told the defendant about his chances for an O.R. release that he agreed to talk to you and made this alleged confession?*
A: *Yes, I believe it was.*
Q: *Thank you, Officer. I believe that will do.*

Once again, the officer could have done himself and his credibility a favor if he had only listened to the tape before getting on the stand. Several months after you've said something, don't stick your memory out on a limb unnecessarily if you've got something around to refresh it—like photos and tape recordings. Know what's in them *before* you get asked about them.

☐ EXAMINE PHYSICAL EVIDENCE

Everything I've just said about reports, pictures and tapes applies to other evidence, too. Make sure you know exactly what you've got. Don't be like the cop who swore his initials were on a label on the blood vial, but then couldn't find them; or the cop who said he recovered a Sony TV, then brought in a Sanyo; or the cop who described a .38 Smith and Wesson, then reluctantly identified a .38 Colt. Check it over before taking the stand.

☐ REVISIT THE SCENE

If you're subpenaed to testify in a case where the layout of a building or an intersection or some geographical feature is going to be critical (such as murders, vehicular manslaughters, hostage kidnaps, and any case with a shooting), go back and look it over the day before trial. (If you haven't already done so during your investigation, take appropriate photographs of the area if you need them to help describe the layout in your testimony.)

If you don't include this step in your preparation, this is another area where the defense attorney will be several steps ahead of you. Even something as routine as a DUI arrest can go down the tubes if you're weak in your description of the scene.

One of my first drunk driving trials as a prosecutor looked so *good* in the officer's report, and turned out so *bad* during cross-examination of the cop, that it was hard to believe it was the same case. The jury told me they were largely influenced in their vote of "not guilty" by the fact that after the cop testified so definitely about the street markings and intersection controls, he then admitted (after seeing photos of the area presented by the defense attorney) that he was completely wrong.

If you can reasonably anticipate that you'll be asked questions about distances and relative locations of a particular scene, you should make the minimal effort of driving by it on your way to the courthouse. Even if you've driven the area a thousand times before, at least run by and take a few mental pictures for yourself. Don't let the defense attorney make an unwilling assistant out of you.

□ CONSULT WITH THE PROSECUTOR

Call and see if there's anything in particular the prosecutor wants you to do in preparation for the trial. He may want you to measure something, or get an aerial photo, or interview a doctor, or bring a particular book or training memo with you, or any number of other things.

This may also be his only chance to discuss your testimony with you in any detail before you get to court. His pointed questions may bring out areas where your memory is hazy or your investigation weak, and give you an opportunity to be thinking about your expected testimony. Once in awhile your exchange with the trial prosecutor may reveal an unexpected problem with the case that requires his obtaining a continuance, or perhaps indicates to him that a trial would be a waste of time.

The larger the city or county where you work, the tougher it will be to get together with your prosecutor ahead of time. But you should always try, and you should be especially persistent about reaching him in serious felony cases. Ideally, you and the prosecutor should not first meet each other in the trial court as you come forward to be sworn in. You can bet that the crook and his lawyer will have talked the case over; you and *your* lawyer should do no less.

□ MAKE AIDS

Nobody can get up on the stand with a perfect recollection of every detail of an isolated case that took place months or years earlier. Nobody should try. You just wind up doing a lot of guessing, or you sound like you're reciting the Gettysburg Address.

On the other hand, you simply can't afford to leave anything out. If you do, you leave yourself wide open to impeachment, as I discussed a few pages back. So what you have to be sure you take into the courtroom with you each time you go in are three important things: your memory, your common sense, and testimony aids.

Your testimony aid may only be your copy of the traffic ticket with a few notes on back. It may be a copy of your report. Or it may be something you've prepared especially for *this* trial, or *this* hearing.

In those cases where the judge or jury needs a *diagram,* for example, you should either draw a large one in advance, or draw a small (but detailed) sketch on a piece of paper and carry it with you to court. You can use your small sketch both as a reference for an in-court drawing of a larger diagram, and as a reference for refreshing your recollection during your oral testimony.

Another kind of testimony aid is some kind of memory "key" you keep in your head. For example, I recently used an officer in a suppression motion where the pivotal issue was the officer's probable cause to arrest a man for being under the influence of heroin. In his report, the officer (who had more than six years experience) included, at various places throughout his narrative, all of these facts:

- Defendant was a known addict.
- The area was a known narcotic traffic center.
- Defendant turned and ran as the police car came into view
- Moments later, the officer saw defendant standing on a sidewalk, swaying from side to side.
- Defendant frequently glanced up and down the street.
- He continually rubbed his face, near his eyes.
- When the officer walked up from behind and defendant turned to face him, defendant's pupils were pinpointed.
- His speech was slurred.
- There was no odor of alcohol on his breath.
- His hand movements were slow and clumsy.
- His eyelids were droopy.

Based on the officer's training and experience at recognizing these symptoms of opiate influence, he had plenty of probable cause for the arrest. But during my direct examination of the officer, he either became nervous or awfully forgetful, because the following problem developed after he had testified as to the first *five* of the facts listed above:

Q: *(By D.A.) Did you see anything else that you thought was significant?*
A: *Yes, sir.*

Q: *What was that?*

A: *He was continually rubbing his face, around the eyes, with both hands.*

Q: *Why did you think that was significant?*

A: *Because I've often seen people do that, who were later determined to be under the influence of heroin.*

Q: *Did you see anything else that you considered significant?*

A: *(Pause.) No, that was it.*

Q: *What happened next?*

A: *I placed him under arrest and put him into my police unit.*

Q: *Other than the six things you've already testified to as being significant factors in your decision to arrest Mr. Perez, do you remember anything else you saw that you relied on in deciding to make the arrest?*

A: *No, sir.*

(See the problem? He's completely left out five other factors that are included in his report! That made it necessary for me to jog his memory.)

Q: *Officer, it's been five months since you made this arrest—were most of these things fresher in your memory then than now?*

A: *Yes, sir.*

Q: *While the facts were fresh in your memory, did you write a report about them?*

A: *Yes, sir.*

Q: *Did you try to include in your report all of the facts you relied on in deciding to arrest Mr. Perez?*

A: *Yes.*

Q: *Do you have a copy of your report with you?*

A: *Yes, I do.*

Q: *Do you think you remember, without looking at your report, everything that you recorded there?*

A: *I'm sure I can't remember everything.*

Q: *Would looking at your report refresh your recollection as to all of the observations you had made before you arrested Mr. Perez?*

A: *I'm sure it would, yes.*

Q: *Please take a look at page two—(pause)—now, does that refresh your recollection?*

A: *Yes, it does.*

Q: *And do you now remember anything else that you had noticed about Mr. Perez before you made the arrest?*

A: *Yes, sir.*

And then, of course, we got the rest of the P.C. in. That wasn't so bad. What was bad was that by now the officer's ability to recall *other* things had been cast in doubt. If we had been in a jury trial with that kind of problem, it could really have hurt.

How simple could a memory aid be for this kind of problem? As simple as the number 11. If the cop had entered the courtroom with the number 11 in his head, things would have gone a whole lot easier.

In his report, this officer described eleven different factors which contributed to his P.C. to arrest Perez. All he had to do was count them off on his fingers as he testified to each one, and he'd have known after the first six that there were still five to go. Or he could even have relied on me to do the counting for him— did you notice?

Q: *Other than the* <u>*six*</u> *things you've already testified to . . .*

The problem was that since he didn't know, going in, how many factors he was going to be listing in his testimony (he told me after the hearing he hadn't thought of *counting* them), he had no way of telling when he had covered them all. He was relying strictly on his memory, and giving it no help, when all it needed was the "key" number 11.

It's possible, of course, that even if he had taken this "key" in with him, he might have gotten stalled after six or seven factors. The difference is that if he <u>knew</u> he still had four or five things to be covered, he could simply say: "Yes. I know I had several other things in my report and I can't recall just now which ones I haven't covered yet."

Then he could refer to his report, refresh his recollection, and fill in the remaining blanks. When your credibility is on the line, that's a whole lot better than getting to number six and then saying: "That's all there was."

Anytime you have a *series* of things you're going to have to recall, make yourself a little memory key—a number, a code word, a poem, a joke—whatever it takes to help you pull every item on the list out of your five-month-old memory.

☐ PREPARE TECHNICAL DATA

If it's reasonable to anticipate that you'll be asked about something too technical to memorize, take written materials with you. For example, in traffic cases you may have to explain how your radar gun works; in DWI cases, you may be asked about the workings of the breathalyzer or intoximeter; traffic accident cases may require some testimony about speeds in feet per second, or standard reaction time, braking distance, and stopping distance, or the timing of traffic signals. And fraud cases may test your understanding of business, financial and data-processing practices.

If you're called as an expert (in handwriting, finger-printing, ballistics, polygraph, criminalistics, narcotics, etc.), you'll be asked extensive questions about your training, experience, readings, special studies, and other qualifications. Recalling every class you've taken and every book you've read gets difficult sometimes. So I suggest you start keeping a record of all your qualifications, and keep it updated, so you can refer to it when you're asked to recite your background. (In Chapter 9, I've covered the typical sets of questions for the various areas of expertise, and I've included a sample outline for your record of qualifications. This record is what you should take to court with you for reference.)

☐ TAKE THE BEST EVIDENCE TO COURT

Some cops remind me of the woman who left her real diamond necklace in the safe and took the glass fake to the jeweler for appraisal. When he told her the necklace was worthless, she said: "Oh, I know that. But how much is the real one worth?" The jeweler asked to see the real one, and the woman told him: "No, I have to keep that one in a safe place . . . just do the best you can with the fake one. After all, it's an exact copy!"

I've had cops come to court with *copies* of forged checks, *copies* of signed confessions, *copies* of handwriting exemplars, *copies* of fingerprint cards, and *copies* of falsified documents. When I asked where the *originals* were, they told me: "Don't worry. I've got them in a safe place in the evidence locker back at the station."

Judges are just like the jeweler: they have to see the real McCoy before they can make a ruling. So they have this law of evidence called "the best evidence rule." It says that with a few specified exceptions (like official government records), a writing can't be admitted into evidence unless it is *the original.* The original doesn't do us any good sitting in the evidence locker— it's got to get to the judge and jury!

The same applies to other forms of evidence you collect. I once had a homicide investigator come to an attempted-murder trial without the knife and bloody clothes. Where were they? "Safe in the evidence locker, but I've got *pictures* of everything."

We're not operating an evidence museum! The purpose of collecting and preserving evidence isn't to keep it safe forever in the evidence locker. The purpose is to introduce it at trial against the defendant. In order to introduce it, we've got to lay it before the court. So when the prosecutor asks you to bring in the evidence, don't take copies or pictures of it—take *the* evidence.

I think it's probably natural for cops to think they don't need to bother with a lot of preparation. The truth is, they do. Depending on the type of case and the particular court, it may cost anywhere from a few hundred to as much as $10,000 a day to operate a courtroom to try the crook you've arrested. And in a great number of cases, *your* performance on the witness stand is going to determine whether a guilty crook goes free after a big waste of everybody's time, energy and money, or whether he goes off to prison for a few years.

You work hard in the field to make the arrest. Don't give it all away for nothing in the courtroom because you "don't need to bother" with preparation. Don't wade into a courtroom fight with the crook unless you're better prepared than he is to win the case. We can't afford to let him have the last laugh.

□

YOUR ROLE
AS WITNESS

Being a cop is something like being an actor, and it's something like being a race car driver: you have to play a lot of different parts, and you're constantly shifting gears. When you're taking a burglary report at a doctor's office, you've got to be clean-cut, intelligent, and perceptive. When you're arresting a drunken legal secretary, you've got to be patient but firm. Interviewing a street-wise dope dealer, you've got to be hip to street slang and as cool as a poker player. You've got to know when to intimidate and when to entice . . . how to command and how to cajole. From traffic accident to rape victim to robbery in progress to family feud, you're constantly slipping in and out of various ratios of gunfighter to peacemaker to child psychologist to sleuth to medic to technician to mechanic to bouncer to public relations expert. And lots more.

Being a cop covers a lot of territory, and you have to adjust continually to the role you're playing. "Witness" is just one more role. It requires a certain approach, a particular demeanor, and a special balance between courtesy and independence. Cops who haven't acquired an appreciation of the requirements of being a witness usually have a tough time on the stand, and don't make very good witnesses for the prosecution. (Which means they make pretty good witnesses for the defense.)

So as you leave the field and open the courthouse door to go inside, don't forget to shift gears. You're changing from *enforcer* to *witness*. Your approach to your duties has to change accordingly. Here are some things to keep in mind.

YOU'RE ON DISPLAY

There are all kinds of people in the courthouse who may have something to do with your case. Anyone you see, or anyone who sees you, could turn out to be a judge, a clerk, a bailiff, a juror, a defense investigator, or a defense witness. If you say or do the wrong thing near these people during the time you're in and around the courthouse (before, during, or after trial), you could wreck the case.

So be on your best behavior. If you're standing around the hallway joking with other cops about dusting someone or busting some guy's face, you may be overheard by someone who turns up in the jury box on your case of resisting arrest, and you can probably kiss it goodbye.

Or if you're overheard talking about the terrible hangover you've got from last night's choir practice, you may be spinning your wheels when you start testifying about what a horrible drunk driver the defendant was.

And anything you say about the particular case you're appearing on could later be grounds for a mistrial if a juror admits he heard you discussing the case outside the courtroom. So try to follow these precautions:

1. Be polite to everyone you come in touch with in the courthouse.
2. Treat all civilians as if they are potential jurors on your case.
3. Don't discuss inflammatory or private aspects of your official duties or personal life where you might be overheard.
4. Don't discuss controversial subjects (like politics, religion, or public issues) where you might be overheard.
5. Don't discuss *anything* about the case you're appearing on where you might be overheard.
6. Don't exhibit unconcealed evidence where potential jurors or defense personnel can see it. If you have something too big to put in a brown bag (like a shotgun or bloody bayonet), make arrangements ahead of time to store it in the prosecutor's office or the judge's chambers. If this presents a chain-of-evidence problem, you may have to wrap it in brown paper or put it in

a cardboard mailing tube. (Be careful not to contaminate.)

7. Don't allow the defendant, his attorney, or defense witnesses to engage you in an argument. It is best to avoid defense personnel completely around the courthouse if you can. If the defense attorney wants to question you about the case, you can politely tell him you don't think the hallway is an appropriate place for discussion, and suggest the prosecutor's office instead.

8. Dress appropriately. As a tactical matter, your prosecutor may want you to appear in uniform or in a business suit, depending on the case. If the case is resisting arrest, for example, and you know that the defense is going to be: "This big Nazi cop attacked me with guns and clubs and mace, and I had to defend myself," don't parade into the courtroom in full uniform, with hip motorcycle boots, a crash helmet, dark glasses, and a waistband full of guns and clubs and mace. A conservative suit would be much better.

And if you've gotten a little thick around the waist and don't look too striking in your uniform, you may want to wear loose clothing to court. Even though the jurors may sit around watching TV at night, drinking beer and getting fat, they expect their police officers to stay lean and agile. Try to look as lean and agile as you can.

YOU'RE ON DISPLAY . . .

When you take the oath and get on the witness stand, you're under the jury's microscope. Remember to dress appropriately, be prepared to testify accurately, and treat courtroom personnel courteously.

The impression you give the judge and jury from the way you conduct yourself in court can go a long way toward enhancing the credibility of your testimony.

9. Female and minority officers still seem novel (and maybe a little inferior) to some people. If you fit into these categories, don't make matters worse by coming on like you've got something to prove. Just be yourself. Don't you be the one to make an issue of your sex or race.

10. Be punctual. It doesn't help the cause much if you keep the judge and jury waiting after the lunch recess, especially if they all hurried to get back on time.

11. Know your way around. If you haven't been to a particular court before, ask the prosecutor where he wants you to wait until you're called, and where you should stand to be sworn in. The area directly in front of the judge's bench is forbidden territory. Don't walk through it to get to the witness stand.

Remember that the impression you make on the judge and jury before you ever open your mouth to answer the first question may have a lot to do with whether or not they *believe* your testimony.

KEEP YOUR PURPOSE IN MIND

Your purpose in getting up on the witness stand and answering questions is to try to put the judge and jury back at the scene of the crime and arrest. The better you are at doing that, the more likely it is that the evidence will convict the criminal.

Don't be confused. It isn't the purpose of your testimony to convict the defendant (we'll let *the facts* do that). And it isn't the purpose of your testimony to defend what you did *(the facts* will do that for you). And it isn't your purpose to help the prosecutor win and the defense lawyer lose (that's up to *the facts,* too). Your purpose in testifying is to draw, as completely and accurately as possible, a word-picture that will allow judge and jury to "see" and "hear" what *you* saw and heard at the crime scene.

Look at it this way: if the judge and jury had been with you when you made the arrest, they'd find the defendant guilty without any problem, right? That's what we're trying to accomplish with your testimony. We want to put the jury into a time machine; take them back to the night of the arrest—let them ride along in your patrol car and see the defendant's car weaving up ahead; watch it go all over two lanes of the road; see how he fails to respond to the red and blue lights and siren; see how he finally pulls off the road and parks crookedly; watch him fall out of the car and stumble back to you; smell his breath; hear his slurred speech; see his bloodshot eyes; watch him fumble for his license; see his miserable performance on the field sobriety tests; and listen to his tirade of profanities as you hook him up and haul him away.

That is the purpose of your testimony. Once the jurors have seen and heard and smelled the same things you did, we've got our guilty verdict in the bag.

If you approach your role as witness with the idea that you're there to convict the defendant, that's going to show through in the answers you give, the way you react to the prosecutor and defense attorney, and even the tone of your voice. And you're going to lose credibility with the jury the minute they sense that you're "out to get the defendant."

But if you approach your testimony with the objective of taking the judge and jury back with you to see what happened—and you're content to let the case rest on what you show them—you're not going to run any risk of betraying a bias in your testimony.

Except for being more restricted by the rules of evidence and procedure, a trial is a lot like your field investigation. When you get to the scene of a traffic accident or an auto theft or a murder, you line up the witnesses, and one by one you make them reconstruct the crime for you—you make them take you back to see and hear what they saw and heard, so you can figure out what happened. When you question the witnesses, you want them to be as accurate as possible. You don't want them to choose up sides and try to slant their statements in favor of or against anyone—you just want to know what happened, and the *facts* will tell you who was at fault and who should be arrested.

It's the same at trial. If all the prosecution witnesses are obviously trying to get the defendant convicted, and all the defense witnesses are obviously trying to get him off, it's hard for *either* attorney to go to the jury and argue that *his* witnesses are more believable. We can

Take the jury back to that day . . .

. . . or night, and show them what happened.

always count on one thing: the defendant and his witnesses *are* going to be obvious in their bias. So if the prosecution witnesses (including you) show that they're content to have the case judged on an unbiased account of the facts, we're going to have one very big edge in the credibility contest.

There are some tell-tale indications of an officer who doesn't have the right purpose in mind when he testifies. The jury notices these signs, and in case they don't, you can bet the defense attorney will point them out. So *you* have to be aware of them and make sure they don't creep into your testimony.

1. You're not an advocate—you're a witness. Don't try to help the prosecutor. Don't try to thwart the defense lawyer.
2. You're not "in league" with the prosecutor. You're in court because you got a subpena, and you came in to tell what you know about the case.
3. Don't be any more or less courteous to the defense lawyer than to the prosecutor. Some officers are so obvious as to stop smiling and brace themselves in the witness chair when the court announces cross-examination, and their tone changes from cordial to hostile when they begin to answer defense questions. There should be no visible and no audible changes in your testimony and demeanor when the case goes to cross-examination.

4. Some cops think it's their job to be as uncooper-
   ative and antagonistic to the defense attorney as
   possible. In fact, all this does is to play into the
   defense lawyer's hands, allowing him to argue to
   the jury later that the officer was obviously
   motivated in favor of the prosecution and didn't
   want to answer defense questions; therefore, he
   must have been trying to conceal something
   from the jury and can't be trusted.

Don't try to kid anybody. If you made the arrest
on the defendant, you have an interest in the outcome
of the trial. You're not in the business of arresting
innocent people. And once the jury knows all the facts,
you're confident they'll reach the right verdict. But it
isn't *you* that's going to convict the defendant—it's *the
facts* of what he did. When you arrested him, you were
the enforcer. In court, you're just a witness as to what
you saw, heard, smelled, etc.

So if the defense lawyer asks whether you care how
the case turns out, don't lie and say you don't. You <u>do</u>,
or you wouldn't be human. Say so:

*Of course I care. If I didn't expect the criminal
justice system to confirm that my arrests were valid
by finding that the people I've arrested had com-
mitted the offenses I'd arrested them for, I'd be an
idiot to stay in this job. But I try not to let that
expectation influence the accuracy of my testimony.*

That should hold the defense lawyer who thinks he's going to show you're either a liar, a robot, or an apathetic cop.

BE NATURAL

Believe it or not, everybody in the courtroom is just another human being. The judge, the jury, the lawyers—they're all just common people. So there's nothing to get tense or nervous about when you go to court. We're all just people. Relax. Be yourself.

Some officers (and most other witnesses as well) think they have to show off their college vocabulary while they're on the witness stand. Don't do it. Chances are, at least half of the people in the jury box won't understand you, and they'll resent you for "talking down" to them. Just talk the same way you normally do (but don't curse). The more human you seem, and the more the jurors can identify with the way you talk, the more faith they'll put in your testimony. On the other hand, the more pompous and insincere you sound, the less likely you are to be believed.

Don't talk in police jargon. Jurors aren't used to it. They'll think you're weird. You see, jurors don't realize that police officers can't *see* anything—they can only "observe;" jurors don't know that cops can't *smell*—they can only "detect an odor;" they don't understand why you can't *get out* of a *car*—that you have to "exit the vehicle;" they don't see why you don't simply *turn on* the red lights and siren—instead of "activating the unit's emergency equipment."

When you testify that you "responded" somewhere, the jury wonders why you didn't just *go*. And they don't see why you can't just *phone* someone, instead of having to "telephonically contact the subject." If you get on the witness stand and start talking like some kind of police-robot dictating machine, the jurors are going to be sitting there saying to themselves: "What's the matter with this guy—he talks awful strange! I don't know whether to believe a word he says—that is, if I knew what the hell he was talking about!"

I've talked to literally hundreds of jurors, after dozens of trials, and one of their most common complaints about police testimony is that instead of using plain talk, cops talk as if all of their testimony was contrived, rehearsed and memorized—all of which tends to make it unbelievable.

One trial I specifically recall involved a couple of tough guys accused of assaulting an officer. With no independent witnesses, the case was a pure credibility contest between the cop and the defendants (who, naturally, told a completely different story).

This is the kind of case where the jury either believes the officer over *two* opposing witnesses, or the case goes down the tubes. And if we lose the criminal case, you can always count on getting a notice in the next day's mail of the civil lawsuit filed against you. So your credibility with the jury is *extremely* important.

But what did this cop get up there and do? Rattled off his answers just like your basic standard-issue police-robot dictating machine. He had "responded to a call . . . alighted from a marked vehicle . . . contacted the subjects . . . subjects became combative and belligerent, initiating a physical altercation . . . during the ensuing struggle, reasonable force was exercised against the subjects," etc. I could practically see the jurors squirm in their seats. I'm sure they could see *me* squirming.

Now, I'm no particular genius at trial tactics. The only thing I could think of was to try to surprise the robot out of him. So after the defense rested, I called the officer for rebuttal. He hadn't been expecting to testify again, so he didn't have any answers ready and translated into robot-talk. He was stuck; he had to resort to plain old everyday English. And what a difference! Now he was *communicating!* Now he was *convincing!* Now, he was credible.

Several jurors told me after convicting the defendants, that it was the officer's rebuttal testimony that turned the trick. Before, they said, he had sounded like he was trying to avoid being specific—as if he himself didn't know what he was talking about. But confronted with the obviously-unexpected rebuttal questions, he came across "like a real human being" (their words), and that made the difference.

So don't let anybody tell you that you're going to look "objective and professional" if you use your best police jargon on the jury. You're just going to look unnatural. Nobody ever benefits from that except crooks. And you don't owe them any favors.

Quick Summary: When you're in the courthouse, you're on display, so dress, act and speak accordingly; approach your role as witness with the purpose in mind of taking that judge and jury on a little time trip to show them what really happened; and remember that the only sure way of keeping the jury with you is to be yourself, reacting and talking the way you naturally do in your everyday conversations.

□

AS A
GENERAL
RULE

There are a few general guidelines that apply in just about every kind of case you may be called to testify in. Every officer should have these basic "do's and don'ts" under his belt before getting on the witness stand.

KNOW YOUR LIMITS

Before you get on the stand, check with the prosecutor about what you may and may not testify to. If a suppression motion has been granted as to something, you can't usually even *mention* that item at trial. If the defendant has already admitted some of the charges, you may not be able to talk about those things. Or if one defendant copped out and implicated his co-defendant, some parts of the admission may have to be left out. And depending on the jurisdiction and the charge, you may or may not be allowed to mention the defendant's record.

These are common examples of restrictions on your testimony. There are others (Miranda, field ID, line-ups, prior contacts, consent issues, knock-notice, search warrants, polygraph tests, etc.). If you violate these restrictions—whether intentionally or inadvertently—a <u>mistrial</u> may result. *Don't get on the stand without talking to the prosecutor first.* If there are any forbidden areas, be sure you know exactly what they are, and be sure you observe them as you testify.

This does *not* mean that you are to give untruthful answers. If the box of ammo you found in the glove compartment was suppressed at a pretrial hearing, but the stupid defense lawyer says: "But, Officer, there wasn't any ammo anywhere in that car, was there?", you tell the truth. If he invites the error, he can't complain about it.

The point is that while neither you nor the prosecutor may make mention of inadmissible damaging evidence, if the *defense* brings it into issue with a direct question to you that can't honestly be answered any other way, you don't have to lie to keep the defendant's secrets.

If you have any questions about some particular evidence in a given case, talk it over with the prosecutor beforehand to find out under what circumstances you might be allowed to refer to it.

"I DIDN'T HEAR"

If you don't hear a question, say: "I didn't hear you," or "I didn't hear all of that." Then, either the lawyer will repeat it on his own, or the judge will direct him to do so. Do *not* say to the lawyer: "Could you please repeat that?" In the first place, it's the <u>judge's</u> function, not yours, to tell the lawyer what to do. What's more, the jurors won't know whether you simply didn't hear the question the first time, or whether you're asking for it to be repeated because you want to stall for time, while you think up an answer.

Jury trials follow Murphy's Law: if anything you say *can* be misunderstood, it *will* be misunderstood. And with some jurors, if anything *can* be construed against the police officer, it *will* be. Don't give them the opportunity by using dangerous Hollywood courtroom talk like "Could you please repeat that?" Just say: "I didn't hear the question."

"I DON'T UNDERSTAND"

If you don't understand a question, don't try to answer it—you may wind up saying something you never intended to say. And *don't* ask the attorney: "Could you please rephrase that?" It may look to the jury as if you didn't want to answer the precise question, so you're trying for a slightly different question.

All you need to say is: "I don't understand the question." Then, either the lawyer will rephrase the question on his own, or the judge will direct him to do so.

"I DON'T KNOW"

If you're asked a question that you don't know the answer to, *don't guess*—your guesswork will come back to haunt you before the trial is over. Say: "I don't know."

"I'M NOT SURE, BUT . . ."

If you *think* you know the right answer to a question, but you aren't positive, make it clear that you're not committing yourself to a certainty: "I'm not sure, but I believe he was wearing a long-sleeved shirt." If it turns out later that he was wearing a t-shirt, the jury can be reminded that you honestly told them you weren't sure about the shirt. But if you stuck yourself out on a limb and said he was wearing a long-sleeved shirt, the defense attorney can pull this one:

> *He told us it was a long-sleeved shirt. We know it wasn't. Was he just as accurate about the <u>rest</u> of his positive testimony?*

"I DON'T REMEMBER"

There's a difference between saying "I don't know" and "I don't remember." You say "I don't know" if you don't now, and never did, know the answer. You say "I don't remember" if you once knew, or may have once known, but can't recall now. Don't confuse these two. And don't guess at things you can't recall; just say: "I don't remember that."

NO HEDGING

Don't stick the hedge-phrase "to the best of my recollection" onto your answers. *Everything* you testify to is to the best of your recollection, isn't it? When you start hedging your answers with that useless phrase, you start sounding like you're losing confidence in your own ability to recall. That's when the jury loses confidence in you, too. If you're sure of an answer, sound like it: "I told him about the chemical test requirement a total of *three* times."

DON'T READ ANYTHING IN

I've often seen cops take in a simple yes-or-no question I had asked, get a puzzled "what-is-he-getting-at?" look on their faces, and get really troubled over how to answer. That's because they were trying to read some big significance into the question that just wasn't there.

For example, to make it clear to the jury that we've come to the end of a series of things, the prosecutor may simply ask: "Was there anything else (that you saw, heard, did, etc.)?" He isn't necessarily trying to nudge you into adding another item to the series. If there wasn't anything else, just say "no."

If the prosecutor *is* trying to get something else out of you, he can always jog your memory with a leading question. Usually, he's just trying to tie up the ends, to make it clear that he hasn't left anything out.

Sometimes, just to show he isn't being one-sided about his presentation of the facts, the prosecutor may ask you questions that will hurt his case. Or he may play devil's advocate if one of your answers doesn't sound kosher. No matter what the impact of your answer is going to be, always answer every question the same way: as directly, as briefly, and as truthfully as you can.

BE UNCONDITIONAL

Some cops seem to like the sound of the conditional word "would." When *I'm* prosecuting a case, I cringe at the sound of it. It's too indefinite:

EXAMPLE

Q: *Who was your partner?*
A: *That would be Officer Hill.*
Q: *What area were you assigned to?*
A: *That would have been the Brookside Area.*
Q: *What all does that cover?*
A: *That would be everything north of Lemon Street.*

You see how awful that is? It sounds like there's some condition that has be be fulfilled before you could say for sure that it *was* Officer Hill, etc. Don't misuse "would" like that. You needlessly reduce the convincing force of your testimony.

BE PATIENT

Don't interrupt the attorney with your answer before he has finished the question. Sometimes, a witness is trying to anticipate the line of questioning, and he starts answering what he *thinks* he's being asked, before the question is complete. Don't do it.

For one thing, you may guess the question incorrectly, and you've already given a wrong answer that you have to go back and change after you hear the end of the question. For another, the jury may not know what the question was going to be. If the attorney never finishes it after you interrupt with your answer, the jury is left guessing and wondering about what your answer meant. Be patient: wait for the question mark before you start answering.

ONE AT A TIME

Don't try to out-talk anyone. If the hearing or trial is being transcribed, the reporter can't accurately take down overlapping voices. That makes it impossible for an appellate court to read the transcript and figure out who was saying what.

Even if there is no reporter, the judge and jurors can't normally follow more than one voice at a time. So don't interrupt anyone, and if anyone interrupts you, stop talking. Your courtesy and the other person's rudeness will stand in sharp contrast for the jury.

DON'T VOLUNTEER

Answer every question with the shortest truthful answer. I'd say about 7 out of 10 officers don't know when to stop talking, and after they've completely answered the question, they keep on volunteering information and tacking on explanations as to why they answered the way they did.

It's up to the *prosecutor* to see to it that all of the right information, and none of the irrelevant and inadmissible material, gets to the jury. If he wants more out of you, he'll ask another question. Don't try to tell everything you know about the case in one answer.

Likewise, don't do the defense lawyer's job for him. Make him ask you what he wants to know. Don't volunteer it.

DON'T BE TOO QUICK

Don't be too hasty in answering. If you're on cross-examination and the defense attorney asks you a simple yes-or-no question, and if you snap your answer off immediately, before the prosecutor has a chance to object to what may have been an improper question, you've already done the damage. Once the jury has heard your answer, it's not going to do any good for the judge to tell them to disregard it.

Give the attorney a second (that's all he needs if he's on his toes) to interpose an objection to the question before you start to answer.

DON'T WAIT TOO LONG

Don't be too *slow* in answering. Don't sit and look at the prosecutor after every defense question to see whether or not he's going to object. Let *him* worry about the objection. If you pause too long before answering defense questions, it may look to the jury like you're having to think up an answer. Just about a second will do it.

DON'T STALL

Don't repeat the question back to the attorney. Again, if you didn't hear it, say so. But don't read it back to see if you understood it right. Some officers do that with every other question, and it becomes pretty obvious they're stalling, trying to come up with an answer:

EXAMPLE

Q: *Were you holding a flashlight?*
A: *Was I holding a flashlight? Yes, I was.*
Q: *In which hand?*
A: *In which hand? Uh . . . the right hand.*
Q: *Then how could you open the door?*
A: *How could I open the door? I put the flashlight down.*

Don't repeat the question. Just answer it.

WHEN OBJECTIONS ARE MADE . . .

If either attorney makes an objection, stop talking and wait for the judge to rule. If the judge says "Sustained," that means there was a valid objection to the question. You aren't allowed to answer. Wait for the next question.

If the judge says "Overruled," go ahead and answer the question.

Sometimes, the attorneys and the judge may get into a prolonged argument about the merits of the objection. When it's all over, if the judge doesn't clearly announce his ruling and you aren't sure which way he decided, ask the judge: "Shall I answer, Your Honor?"

If he tells you to answer but you don't fully remember the question, just say "I've forgotten what the question was," or "I'm not sure I recall the question completely." The reporter will then be instructed to read the question for you, or the attorney will repeat it.

PLAY IT AGAIN

It's possible that during the course of the trial you may be asked the same question twice or more. If so, *don't* preface your second answer with the phrase, "I believe I've already stated . . ." Depending on your tone of voice, that phrase may sound like a cheap attempt to chide the attorney for asking again. It's much better just to answer the question the same way you did before. The jury will notice your consistency; you don't need to announce that you've already given the same answer to the same question.

WORDS AND GESTURES

If your case is being tape recorded or transcribed by a court reporter, you have to remember that only the *sounds* you make will show up on the transcript. That means if you nod or shake your head, nothing will show up. If you hold your hands apart and say: "It was about this long," the transcript won't show whether that was 2 inches or 2 feet.

So any gesture you make in the courtroom has to be described out loud as you do it. When you hold your hands apart to indicate a distance, look and see what the distance is, and then *say* something that the record will pick up: "About this far—I'd say eighteen or twenty inches."

"Uh huh" and "huh uh" are hard for the reporter (and the jurors) to distinguish. So don't talk in grunts. Say "yes" and "no."

BRACKETS WON'T BOX YOU IN

One of the defense lawyer's favorite techniques to destroy your credibility is to try to get you to first commit yourself to something, then later have to admit you could be wrong about it. If you're asked any questions by either attorney that call for *measurements you haven't made,* give yourself some leeway with your answer. And I'm talking about *any* kind of measurement: *distance, time, height, weight, speed, age, color,* etc.

There are two ways to answer these questions: either give an *approximation,* or put your answer in *brackets.*

EXAMPLES

(These examples assume you don't know the precise answer.)

Wrong: *He was 45 feet away.*
Right: *He was approximately 45 feet away.*
Or: *He was 40 to 50 feet away.*

Wrong: *We waited 30 seconds.*
Right: *We waited about 30 seconds.*
Or: *We waited 25 to 35 seconds.*

Wrong: *I'd say he was 5 feet 10 inches.*
Right: *I'd say he was 5 feet 9 to 5 feet 11 inches.*

Wrong: *He weighed 175 pounds.*
Right: *He weighed about 170 to 180 pounds.*

Wrong: *She was doing 75 mph.*
Right: *She was doing around 70 to 80 mph.*

Wrong: *He looked like he was 23 years old.*
Right: *He looked like he was 20 to 25 years old.*

Wrong: *He was wearing black pants.*
Right: *He was wearing very dark-colored pants.*

The less certain you are of your approximation, the *wider* brackets you should give yourself. You may want to bracket someone's height by 2 or 3 inches on either side, or bracket a weight by 20 or 30 pounds. Generally, the larger the numbers you get into, the wider your brackets should be. Total distance of a pursuit might be bracketed in *miles,* whereas the distance of a pace might be bracketed in hundreds of *yards.*

And to help the jury visualize distances under 50 feet, it's a good thing to use courtroom distances for illustration. For example, some jurors don't know how far 20 feet is, so instead of just saying: "It was about 20 feet," point out something in the courtroom that's 20 feet away and say: "It was about from me to that first row of seats there . . . I'd say about 20 feet."

THE I.D.

A special application of the point-and-say procedure is the in-court identification of the defendant. In many cases, identification won't be a major issue in the case, and the prosecutor may get it in summarily like this:

> **Q**: *Officer, did you arrest the defendant here on the evening of September 21, 1979?*

When you answer "yes," the ID is in. But in some cases, mistaken ID may be the whole defense, and the prosecutor will have to be careful not to "lead" you in identifying the defendant (and sometimes, of course, you'll have 2 or more defendants who have to be identified individually). Bearing in mind that there are usually several people in the courtroom near the defendant, or in his direction, and bearing in mind that the transcript only shows what is said aloud, this would be the **WRONG** way for you to ID the defendant:

> **Q**: *Would you recognize him if you saw him again?*
> **A**: *Yes, sir.*
> **Q**: *Is he here in the courtroom?*
> **A**: *Yes, he is.*
> **Q**: *Would you point him out, please?*
> **A**: *That's him right there.*

The **RIGHT** way is to point to him, state where he is in the courtroom, and briefly describe what he's wearing (or other distinguishing features):

Q: *Would you point him out, please?*

A: *That's him, seated at the end of the counsel table, wearing blue jeans and a brown checked shirt.*

Q: *Your Honor, may the record show that the officer has identified the defendant, Frank Nasty?*

The Court: *The record will so indicate.*

YOU'RE NOT THE JUDGE

As a group, judges are pretty egocentric. They resent it if anyone tries to infringe on their authority. So they'll come down pretty hard on you—in front of the jury—if they think you're playing judge. So unless your interpretation of the law is in issue (as in a suppression motion, for example), don't start quoting or interpreting the law. That's the judge's job. He doesn't want the jury getting legal definitions or instructions from anyone but him.

Here's how that works:

Q: *Then you couldn't see the defendant's car until it was within 10 feet of the stop sign?*

A: *That's right.*

Q: *Then you don't know whether she had already stopped back there, and then pulled forward, do you?*

A: *No, but it wouldn't make any difference, because the law requires her to . . .*

The Court: *This court will be the judge of what the law requires, Officer. I think I can do that without your help—just answer the questions!*

You don't need to alienate the judge. And you don't need to have him reprimand and embarrass you in front of everybody. So try not to tug on his robes.

If the defense attorney asks you for a legal conclusion, your prosecutor should object. If he fails to, a good way to respond is like this:

Q: *Well, isn't that exactly what the law provides?*
A: *If you're asking me for a <u>legal opinion</u>, I'll have to defer to the court on that; if you're asking for <u>my understanding</u> of the law, I could tell you what that is . . .*

By now, either your prosecutor will have awakened and made his objection (sometimes, he may want your opinion to come in), or the judge will disallow the question on his own, or the defense lawyer will tell you it's your *understanding* that he's asking for. If nobody objects, go ahead and answer. (An approach like this is the only sure way to avoid offending the judge, even though it's really the lawyer's fault that you're in the predicament.)

If you get the chance, you may want to ask the prosecutor before the trial whether the judge has any idiosyncracies that you should know about. And if you find out about some judge's idiosyncracies the hard way during your trial, don't forget to pass the word to your fellow officers at roll call . . . it may save them an unpleasant experience.

YOU'RE NOT THE JURY

The same guidelines apply. Don't draw the ultimate conclusions of fact for the jury—permit them to do it.

WHO ARE YOU TALKING TO?

Theoretically, all of your answers should be directed to the jury. After all, satisfying the lawyers' curiosity isn't the objective of the trial, and they usually already know most of the answers. But as a practical matter, it looks a little strange for you to face the jury as you answer the lawyers' yes-or-no questions. So I suggest that you direct your short answers to the person who's asking the questions, but when you are *explaining* something (like a patrol procedure, or how to evaluate a hype or lift latents), you should turn and face the jury— explanations are for *their* benefit.

Also, if the lawyer begins his question by saying: "Would you please tell the jury . . . ," you should face the jury with your answer.

If the judge asks you a question, you should turn and face him with your answer. (If this forces you to turn away from the jury, remember to raise your voice enough so they hear you.)

THEY CAN'T SEE THROUGH YOU

If you're explaining something from a blackboard or a diagram, don't stand right in front of it—no one will be able to see what you're drawing or pointing to. Try to stand to the side so that everyone can tell what's going on.

If you're asked to draw a diagram in court, don't talk into the blackboard—no one will understand you. Turn back to face the open courtroom when you speak. (Don't forget to describe your drawing *aloud* for the benefit of the transcript; use letters or numbers to *label* objects, people and routes on your drawing.)

WRITE BIG

Too many cops go up to a 4' blackboard or chart paper and draw a diagram that would fit on this page. Then everyone strains to see it, and the cop strains to find room to draw in all the additional details that the lawyer asks for. Or they draw a street lane 6" wide, and then make the vehicle symbols half an inch wide.

Now, you don't have to take any art courses, and you can't possibly draw everything to scale. But you should generally make diagrams fill the entire space available (unless it's oversized), and you should draw cars and trucks so that they take up most of the lane (as they actually do). Otherwise, your diagram is too misleading and confusing.

Don't waste a lot of time drawing in things that aren't important to the issues in the case (if it's an intersection accident, you don't have to put in every tree, fence and building down the block).

HOLD IT UP

If you're testifying with some evidentiary exhibit— like a gun or knife or blood-stained panties—hold it up where the jury can see whatever you're pointing out. (Obviously, don't point a gun at anyone; it should be kept open, unloaded, and on safety.)

WATCH YOUR PRONOUNS

When you're testifying about things that three defendants and four victims and two witnesses did and said, be careful about saying "he" and "him," etc. If it isn't clear whom you're referring to, the jury will decipher it according to Murphy's Law. Sometimes, the only way to keep it clear is to use names, instead of pronouns:

EXAMPLE

Wrong: Q: *What happened then?*

A: *He told him to hit me and he said that he would if he didn't.*

Right: Q: *What happened then?*

A: *Mr. Reyes told Mr. Benton to hit me, and said that he would do it himself if Mr. Benton didn't.*

Try to draw diagrams that take up all the available space. The bigger they are, the easier they are to see and to work with.

Remember to stand to the side, so you don't block anyone's view. And talk to the people in the courtroom —not to the blackboard.

Also, remember to describe what you're doing so the reporter's transcript will make sense.

BE ANIMATED

Most jurors don't need much of an excuse to fall asleep. Try to avoid a monotone voice. Don't lean back and get too comfortable, or you may give the jury an idea (we also used to have a municipal court judge who regularly fell asleep in trials). Stay alert and show interest in your own testimony (even if it's the 1,284th drunk driving case you've testified in).

BE RESPECTFUL

Always address the judge as "your honor." Don't address him as "Judge Tompkins," or whatever. Try to get in the habit of saying "Yes, your honor," and "no, your honor," instead of "yes, sir," and "no, ma'am." I've seen a few sensitive lady-judges who resented being call "ma'am."

If you need to address the attorneys and don't know their names, call them "counsel." If the defense attorney is an S.O.B., kill him with kindness. Remain respectful.

Don't address the jurors by name while testifying— even if they're your next-door neighbors.

Refer to the defendant as "Mr. Reyes" or "Miss Jackson," etc., even if Reyes is the biggest dirt-bag dope dealer in the state and Jackson has a ten-page rap for prostitution.

BE HUMAN

If something is funny, don't be afraid to laugh along with the others in the courtroom. (But don't sit there with a big grin on your face when there's nothing funny. For the most part, trials are serious matters conducted soberly.)

If you feel a little outraged as you describe how the defendant starved and tortured his infant son, it won't hurt for the jury to see a little controlled outrage in your face (don't overdo it).

If your testimony evokes your feelings of compassion, regret, perplexity, resignation, resentment, conviction, etc., and if it would be normal and human for it to do so, don't worry if a little of that shows through (but don't put on any emotional displays). Although the odds are you're considerably more hardened than the jurors, you still don't want to come off like a robot. You should be restrained, but not indifferent.

WHEN YOU'RE EXCUSED . . .

Unless you're asked to remain, leave the courtroom and go about your duties. If you sit around the courthouse like a vulture, the defense attorney will accuse you of an inordinate interest in the outcome of the trial and will argue that's a motive for you to exaggerate or lie in your testimony.

If you *are* asked to remain, be quiet and attentive. Don't sit there making faces and shaking your head in obvious disagreement with the defense witnesses.

Likewise, don't nod in agreement with other prosecution witnesses.

Don't be whispering continually in the prosecutor's ear. He can't listen to two voices at the same time, and he *has* to know what the witness on the stand is saying. If you want to comment to him on the testimony, write brief notes and give them to him when it won't distract his attention from the proceedings.

BE RESOURCEFUL

Have I covered everything for you? No way. You're going to encounter questions and tactics in every trial that require you to simply keep cool and use your judgment. As with anything else, the more you testify, the better you'll get. And don't forget to share what you learn with other officers, and pump them for any help they can give you. Let's not keep secrets . . . we're all in this business together.

□

LAYING THE
FOUNDATION

The first questions you're going to be asked are called "foundational" questions. They lay the foundation for the rest of your testimony and generally consist of background questions about who you are, what your experience is, and how you happen to be connected with this particular case.

The prosecutor usually uses preliminary questions to establish certain things like the court's jurisdiction over the case, your jurisdiction over the arrest, and any technical elements of the crime that don't require contested proof. He will also ask some questions which "set the scene" for the jury before he gets into the critical issues.

Here is a fairly typical sequence:

Q: *Please state your full name, and spell your last name for the reporter.*

A: *John Clyde Carter, C-A-R-T-E-R.*

Q: *What is your occupation?*

A: *I'm a police officer.*

Q: *Employed by whom?*

A: *By the City of Orange Police Department.*

Q: *How long have you been so employed?*

A: *Approximately three and a half years.*

Q: *Did you have prior law enforcement experience?*

A: *Yes.*

Q: *When and where was that?*

A: *Immediately before joining Orange Police Department, I was with Los Angeles Sheriff's Office for approximately two years as a Deputy Sheriff.*

Q: *Were you working in your capacity as an Orange police officer on Tuesday, June 19, 1979, at about 10:30 p.m.?*

A: *Yes, sir.*

Q: *What was your assignment then?*

A: *I was working patrol in District Four.*

Q: *Where is District Four?*

A: *That's roughly the area north of Kell Creek and east of Lewis Road.*

Q: *Is the intersection of 18th and Vincent within that area?*

A: *Yes, it is.*

Q: *Is that intersection within Orange City limits?*

A: *Yes, sir.*

Q: *And is it within Orange County?*

A: *Yes, sir.*

Q: *On the evening of June 19, were you wearing a distinctive police uniform?*

A: *Yes, I was.*

Q: *Were you using a marked police car?*

A: *Yes, sir.*

Q: *Were you working alone, or with a partner?*

A: *I had a partner.*

Q: *Who was that?*

A: *Officer Nancy Woods.*

Q: *Which of you was driving that night at around 10:30 p.m.?*

A: *Officer Woods was driving.*

Q: *If you recall, what were you doing just prior to 10:30 p.m.?*

A: *We were patrolling northbound on Lewis, near Dana Mall.*

Q: *Did you get a particular radio dispatch then?*

A: *Yes, we did.*

Q: *How was the call dispatched?*

A: *We were assigned a Code 3 to a 901-T, possible fatal, at 18th and Vincent, fire department and ambulance rolling Code 3.*

Q: *In your radio code, what does "Code 3" mean?*

A: *That means it's an emergency call, and we're to go there as quickly as possible, using our siren and red and blue lights.*

Q: *And is that what you did?*

A: *Yes, sir.*

Q: *What does "901-T, possible fatal" mean?*

A: *"901-T" is an injury traffic accident, and they were adding that someone may be dead.*

Q: *And "fire department and ambulance rolling Code 3" means that they are also on their way, with lights and siren?*

A: *That's correct.*

Q: *How long did it take you to get to 18th and Vincent?*

A: *Approximately a minute to a minute and a half.*

Q: *Did you approach the intersection by way of 18th or Vincent?*

A: *We came east on 18th.*

Q: *Where did Officer Woods stop the police car when you arrived?*

A: *In the middle of 18th, just west of Vincent.*

Q: *Did you both get out, then?*

A: *Yes, we did.*

Q: *When you arrived, had either the ambulance or fire department gotten there?*

A: *No, not yet.*

Q: *Did you see any indications that a traffic accident had occurred?*

A: *Yes.*

Q: *What did you see?*

A: *There was a car turned upside down in the middle of the intersection and a pick-up truck with major front-end damage parked within the* intersection. And there was a man lying on the pavement beside the overturned car, with apparent head injuries bleeding onto the street, and dark red stains all over his shirt.

Q: *What kind of car was it that was upside down?*

A: *It was a green, 2-door, 1978 Toyota.*

Q: *What kind of pick-up?*

A: *An off-white or very light-colored 1972 Ford.*

Q: *Other than the person you saw lying on the pavement, did you see anyone else at the intersection when you first arrived?*

A: *Yes, I did.*

Q: *How many people?*

A: *Only one, at first.*

Q: *Was that a man or a woman?*

A: *It was a man.*

Q: *Where was he?*

A: *Kneeling beside the person who was lying on the street.*

Q: *Did you go over to where those two people were?*

A: *Yes, I did.*

Q: *Did you see the face of the man who was kneeling?*

A: *Yes.*

Q: *If you saw him again, would you recognize him?*

A: *Yes, I would.*

Q: *Is he here in the courtroom?*

A: *Yes, he is.*

Q: *Would you please point him out?*

A: *That's him there, sitting at the far end of the table, the man with the mustache and curly hair, wearing a gray suit.*

Q: *Your Honor, may the record show that the officer has identified the defendant, Don Rubright?*

The Court: *Yes, let the record show that.*

This was a felony drunk driving manslaughter trial. No one has gotten into the big issues yet (Was Rubright under the influence? Was he driving? Did he kill someone?), but these foundational questions and answers have set the scene for everyone . . . We all know something about Carter's experience, his partner, and how he got involved in this case. We've gotten inside his car with him at 10:30 p.m. that night, heard the Code 3 dispatch, and seen the accident scene as he saw it when he rolled up. We also know that the defendant was kneeling beside an injured person when the cops arrived. See how the scene is set?

We also know that Carter was within his area of jurisdiction (within his city limits), that the court has jurisdiction (within the county), and we have an in-court I.D. of the defendant.

You might be interested to know that some of the questions asked so far are technically objectionable (a few were "leading," one was "compound," and a couple "assumed facts not in evidence."). That's nothing for you to worry about—let the lawyers worry about the *questions;* you just have to worry about the *answers.* (Most lawyers won't waste time and irritate the court by objecting to foundational questions that don't involve the contested issues.)

If you're being called as an "expert witness," there will be more questions on your background, training and experience. Typical examples are covered in Chapter 9.

For the most part, foundational questions will be like those above. About the only thing you need to remember through this stage is to *confine your answer* to the question asked.

Incidentally, the prosecutor may not want to ask the questions about how long you've been a cop and whether you had prior experience, especially if you've only been a cop for one week and had no prior experience. So let him know in your pretrial briefing what your total experience is. Also, be sure to let him know if there's anything out of the ordinary about your background or the facts of this case, so he can be sure to either ask about it or avoid it, as the circumstances dictate. Try not to surprise him from the stand with anything he doesn't already know.

□

COMMON OBJECTIONS

I'm not going to try to make a trial lawyer out of you in this chapter. You don't need that. But you do need a little understanding of what can go wrong with your answers to make them objectionable. Otherwise, you find yourself trying to answer questions but not being allowed to because of some objection. That gets frustrating pretty quickly. And when the answers that seem okay to you continually get stricken by the judge, you just sit there getting angry, and asking yourself: "What am I doing wrong? Why won't they just let me tell what happened?"

There are at least 44 standard trial objections in most states. We're only going to talk about the 2 that account for upwards of 90% of the problems a testifying officer will have: that your answer is a *conclusion*, or that it is *non-responsive*.

Attorneys have two different ways to try to exclude your answer to a given question. They can *object to the question,* before you ever start to answer; or they can wait until they hear your response and then make a *motion to strike the answer* as being inadmissible.

We've already discussed what to do when there's an objection to the question. Now we've got to concentrate on how to avoid getting all your answers stricken once you get the chance to answer.

HOW TO AVOID CONCLUSIONS

Let's broadly define "conclusion" to include all the other terms you often hear used interchangeably with it: speculation, conjecture, supposition, opinion and guess. By whatever name they call it in your courthouse, it means that the witness is stating as a *fact* something that he *doesn't know* to be a fact. Instead of merely telling what he saw, heard, felt, tasted, smelled, said or did, he's interpreting from those facts to give his *conclusion* as to what those facts mean. Drawing conclusions is the jury's job.

How can you tell when you start straying from facts to conclusions? One way is to listen to the **form of the question.** You know the attorney is asking you to speculate when he starts his questions with these loaded phrases:

Q: *Would you assume . . .?*
Q: *Do you suppose . . .?*
Q: *Don't you think that . . .?*
Q: *Couldn't it be that . . . ?*

Q: *Would you suspect that . . . ?*
Q: *Do you imagine . . . ?*
Q: *Don't you think . . . ?*
Q: *Would you care to hazard a guess . . . ?*
Q: *Can't we safely theorize that . . . ?*
Q: *Wouldn't it be fair to presume . . . ?*
Q: *Don't you surmise that . . . ?*
Q: *Do you view that as . . . ?*
Q: *Isn't it strange that . . . ?*
Q: *Do you find it curious that . . . ?*
Q: *Isn't it just as likely that . . . ?*
Q: *Isn't it logical to infer that . . . ?*
Q: *Doesn't that imply that . . . ?*
Q: *Then for all we know . . . ?*

And the one you're likely to hear most often:

Q: *Isn't it possible that . . . ?*

Now, this isn't a list of every conceivable question that might call for a conclusion from you, but these are the most common. With the exception of the specific instances where your subjective state of mind is important (e.g., when you're explaining your PC to stop a car or detain or arrest someone, or telling why you drew your weapon, or explaining why you took some action that requires you to show your *thinking* at the time), you'll want to answer **all** of these questions pretty much the same way: by refusing to speculate. Here's how:

Q: *Would you assume that the robbery had been planned for some time in advance?*
A: *I don't know.*

> **Q:** *But isn't it fair to infer that that was the case?*
>
> **A:** *I'd rather not speculate about things I don't have any way of knowing.*
>
> **Q:** *Then for all we know, it had been planned for quite awhile, is that right?*
>
> **A:** *I could sit here and offer my own theories about what happened, I guess, but I'd prefer to allow the jurors to draw their own conclusions.*
>
> **Q:** *But you will admit that it's possible?*
>
> **A:** *Sir, I really don't believe I should speculate about what is and what is not possible.*

In real life, I doubt if any prosecutor or any judge would ever let that many questions get to you. That's just an exaggeration to show you different ways of saying the same thing.

You should realize that it takes quite a bit of discipline to resist the temptation to offer your personal interpretations. Most of us are conceited enough to think that we probably see most things a little more clearly than everybody else around us. So there's a very natural tendency to want to offer our special insight, and it's especially strong when you *really do* know more about the case than you're allowed to say (that's almost always). You just have to resist the offer with a polite "no, thank you"—"I'd rather not speculate."

There are times when the *form* of the question looks okay, but it's really calling for information you don't personally know, so again, you've got to control yourself. Look:

Q: *Did the officers on the other side of the house identify themselves and announce their purpose?*
A: *I would have to assume that they did.*

Wrong! You don't have to assume anything. Even if the question looks like an attempt to get you to cast doubt on whether your fellow officers complied with the law or departmental procedure, you don't assume anything! As soon as you start assuming things that tend to support one side of the case or the other, your motives and credibility are in trouble:

Q: *What do you mean, you have to <u>assume</u> that they did—did you hear them identify themselves or not, Officer?*
A: *No, I didn't.*
Q: *Did you hear them announce their purpose?*
A: *No, sir.*
Q: *Then on what basis do you assume that they did these things?*
A: *Because that would be the normal procedure.*
Q: *Do police officers always, and in every case, follow the normal procedure?*
A: *Not necessarily.*
Q: *And of your own personal knowledge, do you know whether these officers complied with the normal procedure in this case?*
A: *No.*
Q: *Well, that being the case, Officer, did you offer us your <u>assumption</u> that they complied because you're trying to help the prosecution's case?*

At this point, your prosecutor is going to object that the last question is argumentative, and the judge should sustain the objection. But the jury's already gotten the point, and your credibility has already suffered.

And now the defense lawyer has one more argument to take to the jury in his closing statement:

> *"Ladies and gentlemen, you saw how the officer was willing to make assumptions that were in the prosecution's favor—assumptions about things he had no way of knowing. How many of his <u>other</u> answers may have been motivated by a desire to help the prosecution case look a little stronger? How much of this officer's total testimony was based on his knowledge, and how much was the result of his <u>assumptions</u>?"*

All the defense attorney has to do is raise a "reasonable doubt" about his client's guilt—and that usually doesn't take too much. Don't help him out—don't offer any assumptions from the witness stand. Limit your testimony to things you *know*.

Another major area of conclusionary testimony is what I call **mindreading**. You can't get inside someone else's brain. That means you don't know for a fact —so you can't testify—as to what someone else *sees, hears, feels, thinks,* or *wants;* and you don't know for a fact what somebody is *trying* to do, or is *able* to do, or whether he is *nervous, excited, angry, scared, happy,* *upset, disturbed,* or in any of the other emotional states that can only be labeled with a conclusion.

EXAMPLES

Q: *What did he do then?*
A: *He looked back and saw my police car and heard my siren, then he decided to speed up.*

Wrong! You can't testify that he *saw* and *heard* and *decided* —not unless you crawled inside his head. Just describe the things you know.

A: *He turned his head back over his right shoulder, facing directly at me. Then he jerked his head forward again, and his car sped up.*

Here's another one:

Q: *What was he doing?*
A: *He was trying to break the window out.*

Wrong again! You don't know *what* he was *trying* to do. All you know is what you saw:

A: *He was kicking the window with both feet.*

And another:

Q: *Please describe his performance on that part of the test.*
A: *He couldn't hold his leg out for five seconds.*

You don't know whether he couldn't, or whether he *chose* not to. What you know is what you saw:

> **A:** *He stuck his leg out and immediately dropped it back down onto the ground.*

Final example:

> **Q:** *What did you notice about him?*
> **A:** *That he was really nervous and scared.*

Those are *conclusions* you drew from something else that you noticed:

> **A:** *I saw his hands trembling and his face sweating, and he kept licking his lips.*

Don't try to testify to other people's states of mind, sensory perceptions, or physical abilities. Your conclusions about these things are inadmissible (with the few exceptions I noted) and just wind up producing objections, motions to strike, judicial reprimands, and defense ammo. Stick to the facts.

Is the word "hell" profanity? Some people think so; some don't. Has a motorist become "belligerent" if he raises his voice and starts spitting on the ground? To some cops he has; to others he hasn't. Is a juvenile suspect "resisting" when he tells you he doesn't want to get into the back of your patrol car? Maybe; maybe not.

"OBJECTION SUSTAINED!
STRIKE THE OFFICER'S REMARKS FROM
THE RECORD."

That's what the jury will hear if you use conclusionary language in your answers. The more often the jurors hear the judge ordering your testimony stricken, the less credence they're going to put in your ability to give a factual account of what happened.

So keep the judge off your back: don't offer your conclusions about things you don't really know.

Got the point? A lot of the words that cops use in their reports and in their testimony are **conclusions**—they apply to things that are really a matter of opinion, or maybe even the whole issue of the trial. Wouldn't it be easy if in a trial for resisting arrest, the prosecutor could put you on the stand, ask you: "Officer, did the defendant resist arrest?", then have you say: "Yes, he certainly did," and then rest the case?

The reason that doesn't work is because your *opinion* on the legal issue is an inadmissible conclusion. You've got to give the jury the *facts* of what happened, and see if *they* come to the conclusion (verdict) that the guy really did resist arrest. So here's a list of *conclusionary* words to <u>stay away from</u> when you're on the witness stand (as well as in your reports):

refusal	assaulted	belligerent
admission	attacked	combative
confession	accosted	obnoxious
denial	confronted	threatening
consent	altercation	offensive
waiver	struggle	abusive
indication	resisted	exigent
profanity	forced	
obscenity	suspicious	
vulgarity	furtive	
deception	strange	
guilt	uncooperative	

You can't start using all those conclusionary words without running into a barrage of objections from the attorney and the judge. So instead, just tell the jury *who did and said what,* and let them draw their own conclusions.

HOW TO GIVE "RESPONSIVE" ANSWERS

Have you heard an attorney make a motion to strike your answers as "non-responsive?" Know what that means? Your answer did not directly respond to the precise question you were asked. Usually, that happens because you're trying to anticipate the attorney's next logical question, and you're volunteering the answer to that one in addition to, or instead of, the exact question you were asked.

In our everyday lives, where we're not subject to the rules of court and the evidence code, we give "non-responsive" answers all the time. Everybody does it, everybody expects it, and no one objects to it:

He: *Do you want to go out tonight?*
She: *I've got a lot of homework to do.*

You see, he asked a yes-or-no question; she didn't say "yes," she didn't say "no," she didn't even say "maybe." Her answer was completely non-responsive. But that's the way we normally talk.

However, in court, you can't talk that way. You have to answer just _the_ question that you're asked—no more, no less. That means you have to pay attention to how the question is framed. The way the question is framed dictates the way you must answer. Here are the possibilities:

YES OR NO?

It sounds so simple when you read in this book that you answer a yes-or-no question with a "yes" or "no" (or one of the responses that may be appropriate, like "I don't know," etc.). But you wouldn't believe how many officers have all kinds of trouble with simple yes-or-no questions in court. Mostly, they try to give too much information when a plain "yes" or "no" is all that's called for:

Q: *Did he perform the alphabet test?*
A: *Yes, twice—but he only went to "G."*

Everything after the "yes" is non-responsive. The officer anticipated the next *three* questions and volunteered the answers. He should have limited each answer to one question:

Q: *Did he perform the alphabet test?*
A: *Yes.*
Q: *How many times?*
A: *Twice.*
Q: *How far did he go correctly the first time?*
A: *To the letter "G."*
Q: *How far did he go correctly the second time?*
A: *Again, to "G."*

You may be asking yourself why its preferable to make the attorney ask each of these obvious questions when the officer could have saved a lot of time by volunteering this information. It's preferable because the attorney has the responsibility of conducting his questioning with precision so as to control the evidence that gets admitted. He can't control it if the witness answers something other than the question the attorney asks.

And it's preferable because when you start volunteering answers to questions you haven't been asked, you're going to cause a lot of objections and motions to strike, and pretty soon the jury's going to think you're an undisciplined rookie who doesn't know how to testify.

So answer yes-or-no questions with a "yes" or "no." Make the attorney ask the next question if he wants to get more information. Although this may sound like advice to conceal information, it isn't—it's a procedural *requirement* for an orderly trial.

Here are a few more examples:

Q: *Did you ask him whose car it was?*

Wrong:
   A: *He told me it was his.*

Right:
   A: *Yes.*
   Q: *Did he answer?*
   A: *Yes.*

Q: *What did he say?*
A: *He said it was his.*

* * *

Q: *Was the odor of alcohol the first thing you noticed?*

Wrong:

A: *The first thing I noticed was his walk.*

Right:

A: *No.*
Q: *What was the first thing you noticed?*
A: *His walk.*

* * *

Q: *Did you tell Officer Cain about that?*

Wrong:

A: *Spencer came up and started talking.*

Right:

A: *No.*
Q: *Why not?*
A: *Because Spencer came up and started talking.*

Every one of those initial questions called directly for a yes-or-no answer. What could be easier than simply answering "yes" or "no," and then waiting for the next question? If you can honestly answer a question "yes" or "no," don't add anything else!

WHERE?

If the attorney asks you a question that starts with the word "where," your answer will be non-responsive if it talks about anything except a *location* (or "I don't know," etc.).

Q: **Where** *was Mr. Schubert?*

Wrong:
A: *I was busy with his wife at that point.*

Right:
A: *I don't know.*
Q: *Why not?*
A: *Because I was busy with his wife at that point and didn't notice him.*

* * *

Q: **Where** *were you?*

Wrong:
A: *I was thinking about calling for help.*

Right:
A: *I was over by my car.*

WHO?

If the question asks "who," your answer will be non-responsive unless you talk about a *person* (if you know).

Q: **Who** *threw the bottle?*

Wrong:
  A: *That happened while my back was turned.*

Right:
  A: *I don't know.*
  Q: *Why not?*
  A: *I didn't see it.*
  Q: *Why not?*
  A: *That happened while my back was turned.*

* * *

Q: **Whom** *were you looking for?*

Wrong:
  A: *I had just heard the broadcast on it.*

Right:
  A: *Luis Rodriguez.*

WHEN?

You have to answer this question (if you know) with a *time*, a *date*, or a *reference* to another event.

Q: **When** *did that happen?*

Wrong:
  A: *I've made a hundred arrests since then.*

Right:

   A: *I can't remember.*

   Q: *Why not?*

   A: *Because I've made a hundred arrests since then.*

* * *

   Q: **When** *did you start inside?*

Wrong:

   A: *I wasn't the first one to go inside.*

Right:

   A: *I went in a few seconds after Officer Dooley went in.*

   Q: *When did <u>he</u> go in?*

   A: *About 10 seconds after we knocked.*

* * *

   Q: **When** *did you book him?*

Wrong:

   A: *We didn't go right over there.*

Right:

   A: *At 10:22 p.m.*

WHY?

To answer this question responsively, you have to give a <u>reason</u> or an <u>explanation</u>.

"JUST ANSWER THE QUESTION, OFFICER!"

If you keep hearing that admonition from a judge who seems to be losing patience with you, chances are you aren't keeping your answers "responsive" to the questions.

Many officers submit to the natural temptation to volunteer things that haven't been asked. If you're going to be a better witness, you have to resist that temptation and confine your answer to the question you've been asked.

Q: **Why** *did you go in without knocking?*

Wrong:
> A: *There are times when you have to do that.*

Right:
> A: *Because I didn't want to give them a chance to flush the stuff.*

Got the picture? If you're asked "how many," you give a number; to "which one," you answer by identifying one; "what color?" calls for a color; "what kind?" calls for a type or category; "how?" calls for an explanation; "how much?" requires a quantity, and so on. Don't start answering these questions with an explanation of why you don't know the answer, or some other volunteered non-responsiveness. Be as direct as you can, and then STOP TALKING.

If you learn to listen closely to what's being asked and confine each answer to the scope of each question, you'll reduce by about 90% the number of times you get interrupted by legitimate objections. That should make your testimony flow more smoothly, which should make it more convincing to the jury.

□

HANDLING CROSS-EXAMINATION

Have you ever been up on the stand testifying for two or three days on cross-examination, really getting worked over by the defense attorney, and wondering how you could get even with him? I used to always sit there and say to myself: "OK . . . he gets the last word in here . . . but just wait til I stop this turkey for drunk driving some night!"

I guess it made me feel a little better for awhile to think I was going to get him in *my* territory someday. Trouble was, it never happened. I eventually realized that it never would. The next time I saw every one of the turkeys was back in *their* territory: the courtroom—and they had me on cross-examination again.

I finally came to the conclusion that the only way I was going to get even with defense attorneys was to beat them at their own game—to be so good on the witness stand that I made *them* hate cross-examination more than I did.

Now, considering what I've said so far about your not being an advocate, just being an impartial witness, you may wonder what there is in cross-examination to get even *for* (especially if you haven't had too much courtroom experience). Remember my telling you that in many of the cases you testify in, *your* testimony will be the determinative part of the case? Since that's true, and since your testimony almost always tends to support the prosecution side of the case, the defense lawyer's most important task is to *destroy your credibility* —to make you look like you're either an incompetent bungler, or a liar, or both.

How does he do that? He attacks you. He tricks you. He outsmarts you. He confuses you. He frustrates you. He annoys you. He probes for your most vulnerable characteristic; if he finds it, he jumps on it with both feet and exploits it for all it's worth.

In putting together his strategy before the trial begins, he starts with the report you wrote. He picks it apart, line by line, looking for conclusions, ambiguities, conflicts, mistakes, incomplete investigation, legal errors—anything he can find to throw back at you when he gets you on the stand. That's one reason it's so important that you write the kind of report that doesn't give the defense lawyer anything to work with, and that you know what's in your report before you take the stand.

Then he files discovery motions to see if there's anything in your personnel file or the department's other records that might give his client a foothold on your credibility: do you have a lot of complaints from citizens for excessive force, or racial comments, or discourteous treatment, or inadequate service? Have you been on mental leave or disciplinary days off? What does your daily activity log show for the date of the arrest?

And does the department have maintenance records on the Breathalyzer or GCI you used that night? How about records of your training to run the machine properly, or to lift latents, or make comparisons, or evaluate hypes?

Sometimes, an attorney may not be as interested in actually *finding* something with his discovery motions as in the *effect* the motions have on you. Long before he ever gets you on the witness stand, he may be able to start getting to you with what you perceive as "bullshit motions." If he pesters you enough before the trial starts, your animosity toward him may show up the minute he begins to question you. Since the jury won't know or understand why you start right off at odds with the nice defense lawyer who just asked you a simple question, you lose a point, and the "nice" lawyer gains one.

Solution: try to take all the nonsense pretrial motions in stride, and don't let the lawyer get the effect he's trying for. If you can't help getting annoyed, at least try not to let it show in your response to the lawyer's courtroom questions. (When I could see that a lawyer was trying to annoy me before trial with a lot of bogus motions, I used to carry a little package of Dramamine tablets and offer him one when he came to the station. When he asked me what I was doing that for, I'd just smile politely and say: "These are good for motion sickness.")

In many cases, you may already have testified at some kind of hearing (suppression, speedy trial, Miranda, preliminary, etc.) before the trial. In those instances, the lawyer will have gone over his notes and any reporter's transcript to see what you said. If you say anything differently at trial, he may have some ammo to shoot at your credibility with.

And during your direct exam, the defense lawyer will be taking careful notes of what you're saying. He's going to ask you many of the same questions, perhaps phrased a little bit differently, and see how your answers compare.

While you're testifying on direct, the defense attorney is likely to object at every opportunity. Partly, he'll be doing that to try to keep out evidence. But he may also be objecting frequently to disrupt your train of thought and to keep you as frustrated and agitated as he possibly can, in the hope of having some negative effect on your testimonial clarity and credibility.

So you see, before you've been asked your first question on cross-examination, the defense lawyer has been busy trying to set you up for a fall. Despicable as you may think it is, that's his job; he's getting paid to ruin your credibility with the jury. He'll do everything he legally and ethically can to accomplish that objective. In the process, he's going to directly or indirectly suggest that you're a poor cop or a poor liar. Since you're neither, that's what there is to get even for.

Now, all this talk about "getting even" may sound a little unprofessional. I don't mean it in any vengeful sense. I simply mean to recognize that contrary to popular belief, cops are human beings. So let's face facts: as much as society demands from you, I don't think anyone expects you to sit on the witness stand like some kind of indentured servant, while your professionalism and your personal integrity are impugned, dumbly falling into every trap the defense lawyer lays for you, and then walking away singing: "Sticks and stones may break my bones . . . "

As a prosecutor, what *I* want from you while you're on the witness stand (and what I hope you want of yourself) is that you be a disciplined human being: intelligent, alert, and helpful; confident, but not cocky; courteous, but not fawning; knowledgeable, but not egotistical; firm, but not dogmatic; concerned, but not overly-emotional; restrained, but not indifferent; interested, but not overly-biased; professional, but not overbearing.

Think that's asking too much of a human being? Sure it is. You don't necessarily *achieve* it; you just *aim* at it. That's enough. And that's how you get even—by being *so good* on the witness stand that the defense lawyer has to look someplace else for a hole in the prosecution case. When you've become such an **informed** and **disciplined** witness that the defense attorney sees he's helping the prosecution and hurting himself with every additional question he asks you, he's going to stop asking. And when he has to stop his cross-examination without getting what he wanted out of you, you got even. And then some.

I said you need to be disciplined and informed. By "disciplined," I mean that you keep your cool— stay level-headed, no matter how hard the defense lawyer tries to shake you. Keep your answers responsive, no matter how strong the temptation to volunteer explanations. Be patient, no matter how tedious the questioning becomes. Be consistent, no matter how many times you're asked the same question ten different ways. And be courteous, no matter how obnoxious the defense lawyer and his criminal client may be.

I can't give you this discipline in a book. You have to make it a feature of your own self-control. I've tried to give you some *motivation* for it by pointing out that it's the only way you're going to outsmart the defense lawyer. If my lecturing to you doesn't motivate you to strive for greater discipline, you may have to wait for a tsunami wave. (And if you stay in law enforcement *without* that discipline, it's just a matter of time.)

What I *can* do in a book is to help you be better **informed** as to what to expect on cross-examination, and how you can handle it.

YOU'RE NOT A MOUTHPIECE

Don't let anybody—either lawyer or the judge—put words in your mouth. Sometimes a question sounds like a statement with a question mark on the end, and if it seems 99% accurate, some witnesses take the easy way out and go along with it, even if that's not the way they'd have answered on their own. Don't do it. Don't let anybody suggest something that sounds reasonable and logical and get you to agree to it if you don't *know* that it's 100% correct.

Don't get in a hurry. Take time to be precise. If something in the way a question is phrased is just a little bit wrong, your answer should be: "Not exactly," or "That's *almost* correct," or "With one exception," or some other such qualifier. Let the jury and the prosecutor know you're not buying the whole thing, as is.

One technique a defense attorney can use while cross-examining you is to act like he's asking you some unimportant background questions, and that he's in full agreement with everything you say (nods his head and smiles at you), when he's really trying to get you to buy something that he knows is just a little bit different from what you said in your report, or at the prelim, or on direct at the trial. The little bit of difference seems trivial or just semantical to you, so you go ahead and buy it.

The defense attorney then quickly but smoothly changes the subject to steer you away from the "trivial" difference, and he puts that slight inconsistency in his hip pocket. If he collects a pocketful of such slight inconsistencies from you during the course of cross-examination, he's going to pull them all out at the close of the trial, after you've left the stand and have no opportunity to clarify what you meant. He's going to put them all up on a chart for the jury to look at, and he's not going to make them look so trivial. He's going to argue that you'll agree to just about anything anybody says—even if it conflicts with something else you'd already testified to. "Now ladies and gentlemen, is <u>that</u> the kind of testimony you want to convict somebody on?"

WATCH OUT FOR BLUFFS

Sometimes the defense attorney may try to shake your confidence in your own answers by pulling a bluff. He usually does that by asking a question about something that's in obvious and direct conflict with something you've said, and acting as if he knows it's true, and will be able to prove it later on. He makes it appear that he's caught you in an error and is giving you a chance to recant your former, erroneous testimony before he proves you wrong.

If a cop isn't too sure of his own testimony, the bluff will usually bring that out. He'll start backing down, hedging his original answer, and looking for a way to salvage his credibility.

EXAMPLE

Q: *Do you remember anything unusual about the defendant's eyes that night?*

A: *No, sir.*

Q: *Let me ask you this: as you look at the defendant here in the courtroom today, is there anything different about the appearance of his eyes—different from the way they appeared that night?*

A: *Nothing that I can tell, no sir.*

Q: *Well, now, Officer, then you don't recall the defendant wearing a black eyepatch over his left eye that night?*

A: *I don't recall that, no.*

Q: *Now, Officer, I realize it's been a few months since the night of the arrest. How positive are you that the defendant was <u>not</u> wearing an eyepatch over his left eye?*

A: *I wouldn't say I was <u>positive</u>; I can only say that if he was wearing one, I don't <u>recall</u> that.*

Q: *Then he may have been wearing an eyepatch, and you just don't recall it now—is that what you're saying?*

A: *That's right.*

You see what happened? There never really was any eyepatch. But it sounded *so specific* ("over his <u>left</u>

eye"). And the tone of the defense attorney's voice seemed to suggest that he was going to be able to prove there *was* an eyepatch. And he even helped out with an understandable excuse for the officer's poor memory ("it's been a few months"). And after all, an eyepatch is such an obvious thing that an officer who didn't notice and remember *that* couldn't hope to be believed in the rest of his testimony.

So to play it safe, the cop hedged. He backed down. He took the escape route that the helpful defense attorney was offering: maybe there *was* an eyepatch, and he just didn't recall it now. CRASH! Officer falls into trap.

Is the defense attorney going to call the defendant to testify there was an eyepatch? No. He's simply going to wait until it's time to argue to the jury about the officer's credibility, and then he's going to say something like this:

> *Take this business about the eyepatch. There never was any eyepatch—I never said there was. I just used a hypothetical to see if we could find out how sure the officer was about the things he testified to. I was just testing his memory, ladies and gentlemen, and* <u>look what we found out</u>: *the officer's memory wasn't very good, was it?*
>
> *I mean, something as obvious as an* <u>eyepatch</u>, *for goodness sakes! I didn't ask the officer what color* <u>socks</u> *the defendant was wearing or some detail like that, that a person might not notice.*

I asked whether the defendant was <u>wearing an eye-patch</u>—something unusual—something remarkable. And yet the officer wasn't even positive about <u>that</u>—said the defendant <u>may</u> have been wearing one, and he just <u>didn't recall</u> it now!

Is a witness who can't remember whether somebody's wearing something as distinctive as an eyepatch likely to be very accurate in the smaller details of his testimony? Of course not! That's just one more reason why I submit to you that this officer was a totally unreliable witness. You just can't count on anything he said! If <u>he</u> wasn't sure of it, how in the world can <u>you</u> be sure about it?

Okay. See how the damage gets done? To keep from helping the defense attorney make a monkey out of you, you've got to know what you're talking about, not testify to anything you *don't* know, and not start back-pedalling when the defense lawyer pulls a bluff on you.

DON'T QUANTIFY BRAIN CHEMISTRY

Another defense technique is to try to get you to put numerical values on your thought process. Don't do it. Since you don't really have any basis for doing it correctly, it can only lead to problems.

EXAMPLE

Q: *Officer, you've testified to a dozen or so observations that you made before placing the defen-*

dant under arrest for driving under the influence. Had you already decided you were going to arrest him the minute you stopped the car?

A: No, sir.

Q: Then these observations you say you had made about his driving—these things hadn't totally convinced you that you had an intoxicated driver on your hands before you ever made the carstop?

A: No, sir.

Q: But I take it you were somewhat suspicious that it might turn out that way?

A: Yes, sir.

Q: Then would you say you were about 15% convinced just from the driving pattern that this was an intoxicated driver up ahead?

A: You might say that, yes.

Q: After you saw Mr. Clark stumble back to you and drop his wallet in the mud, did your suspicions increase?

A: Yes, they did.

Q: Say, 25% convinced?

A: I guess so.

Q: And after you smelled the odor of alcohol, saw his eyes, and heard his speech, were you even more convinced—say perhaps 35%?

A: Yes, sir.

Q: Well, Officer, at what point would you say you became at least 51% sure that in your opinion, you were going to arrest this man for driving *under the influence?*

A: *I'd say it was after the field sobriety test.*

Q: *You said there were five parts to that test—was it after the first part, or the third, or just where?*

A: *After the complete test.*

Q: *Not after the fourth part, but after the fifth, then?*

A: *That's right.*

Q: *Now, you said the fifth part was the heel-to-toe walk, I believe. Just exactly what was it in that part of the test that convinced you he needed to be arrested for DWI, even though you weren't yet 50% sure after the fourth part of the test?*

A: *I don't understand your question.*

Q: *As I understand your testimony, Officer, you saw this man driving all over the road at seventy miles an hour; you saw him stumble as he walked; his eyes were bloodshot and watery; his speech was slurred; he stood there and dropped his wallet in the mud; he failed the finger-to-nose test; he failed the alphabet test; he failed the stand-at-attention test; and he failed the one-leg balance test; and after all these things, you <u>still</u> hadn't decided to arrest him; but suddenly, after he failed the heel-to-toe test, you made up your mind. If all these <u>other</u> things hadn't convinced you, Officer, what was it about the heel-to-toe test that made up your mind for you?*

How do you answer that question? You have just helped this lawyer do three things that are going to work to the defendant's advantage.

(1) You've put percentages on the various pieces of evidence we have—you've said the stumbling and dropping of the wallet were worth 10% of a decision. That means that if the defense can explain away these two pieces of evidence ("old war injuries" is always effective), the defense lawyer can tell the jury to subtract 10% of the proof. And so on, until he gets them down to some number he feels comfortable with.

(2) You've made it look like the heel-to-toe test was the critical, convincing factor for you. So if the defense can explain away just that *one* factor, they can make it look like the rest is insufficient to support a guilty verdict—after all, all those other things combined hadn't convinced *you* the guy was drunk.

(3) Worst of all, you've helped the defense attorney instill in the minds of the jurors the notion that you made your decison to arrest on a 51% certainty. Jurors are all instructed that a 51% certainty is NOT beyond a reasonable doubt. Therefore, the defense attorney can simply leave the jury to dwell on your 51% figure when they deliberate, with the good possibility one of them will point out to the others that your decision to arrest fell short of the "beyond a reasonable doubt" standard. (Since your standard to arrest is only "probable cause" —not "beyond a reasonable doubt"—the jurors would be committing a logical error in confusing the two. But that's what jurors often do best . . . remember Murphy's law.)

I don't see how anybody can honestly put percentages on brain chemistry. The process of coming to a decision is brain chemistry. How can you say when you're 28% convinced? Or 63% convinced? You can't. So don't. And if lawyers ask you to, just tell them you can't:

Q: *Would you say you were about 15% convinced just from the driving pattern that this was an intoxicated driver up ahead?*

A: *No, sir, I wouldn't say that at all.*

Q: *Then were you less than 15% convinced at that point?*

A: *I wouldn't say that, either.*

Q: *Well, can you give us a percentage that you think correctly corresponds to your degree of suspicion at that point?*

A: *No, sir. I certainly can't.*

Q: *Why not?*

A: *Because I don't know how to do that. I don't have any built-in reference points that enable me to tell when my mind has passed the "10% suspicion mark," or the "90% certain mark," or anything like that, so I don't know how I could honestly quantify my relative mental states for you.*

Q: *Well, let me put it this way: at what point did you finally make up your mind that you were going to arrest Mr. Clark?*

A: *I don't know.*

Q: *You don't know when you made up your own mind?*

A: *Of course not.*

Q: *What do you mean "of course not?"*

A: *I mean that arriving at a decision is sometimes a gradual, continuing process. I couldn't tell you at what point I decide that I dislike a new song, or like a new friend, and I don't have any kind of mental device that I'm aware of that pops up and tells me I've just come to a decision to arrest someone. So I don't have any basis for answering that kind of question.*

Q: *Well, but I take it from the fact that you didn't arrest the defendant until after the fifth field sobriety test, that you hadn't fully decided to arrest him until after that?*

A: *Not necessarily.*

Q: *You mean you might continue to run a person through parts of the test even after you've already determined to arrest him?*

A: *Yes, sir. I might.*

Q: *Why on earth would you do that, Officer? Is that just to collect more evidence against him?*

A: *There are several reasons why I might do it. I do try to collect as much evidence for the jury as I can, but I don't know ahead of each test whether a person's performance is going to be evidence against him or evidence for him—that depends on how he does.*

And since I make dozens of these arrests a year, I like to try to evaluate each individual suspect on the <u>same basis</u> as all the others. So I try to give them all the same tests. I couldn't do that if I arrested one man after the <u>first</u> test, and another after the <u>third</u> test, and so forth. I try to keep the field sobriety evaluation uniform for everyone.

Did the defense attorney make any mileage this time? Not an inch. No numbers to play with. No percentages to distort. No brain analysis to box the officer in with. No foothold here.

By the way, as you read the lengthier responses above, you may have been wondering about my advice on volunteering explanations. These explanations weren't *volunteered*—they were *asked for* in the questions ("Why not? What do you mean by that? Why on earth . . . ?"). And at least two of them were purposely provoked by the officer so he *could* explain ("I certainly can't" and "Of course not" are a couple of the "unexpected qualifiers" I mentioned in Chapter 2 that you can usually count on to provoke the defense attorney into *giving* you the chance to explain). That's not the same thing as trying to explain in response to a question that doesn't call for any explanations.

<u>BEWARE THE MINUTE OF SILENCE</u>

We've already talked about the dangers of committing yourself to some definite measurement when you should be approximating or bracketing. Another way the defense attorney uses your carelessness against you is to demonstrate for the jury how <u>unlikely</u> your careless testimony is. After he's asked you, for example, <u>how long</u> some event took, and you've given an everyday kind of careless response, "A minute or two," he's going to have a minute or two of silence.

He's going to hold up his watch, and keep the courtroom sitting there in dead silence for one or two minutes, and it's going to seem like forever! A minute is longer than a moment. When you're sitting there in a silent courtroom, a minute is a *long* time.

And you're not the only one who's going to notice how long it is. The jurors will get quite an impression from it, too. Then, if you <u>change</u> your testimony and say the event didn't take *that* long, that it must have just been 5 or 10 seconds, the lawyer pockets another inconsistency in your testimony.

Incidentally, the same thing happens if you get careless in your *report*. You're going to be tied to whatever you've said there, and you're going to be living with it in court. So when you start to write "a minute" in your crime or arrest report, remember the minute of silence. Don't say "minute" if you mean "seconds."

JOHNNY CARSON'S EARLOBES

If ID of the defendant is a big issue, as it often is in armed robberies and rapes, and in cases where several defendants were arrested at the same time (gang fights, for example, or dope raids), a favorite game of the defense attorney is to <u>hide</u> his client before you're called to the stand (assuming you are the ID witness). Before he brings the defendant out to confront you, he runs you through a series of ridiculous questions about the defendant's features, including these:

Q: *What color is the defendant's hair?*

Q: *How long is it?*

Q: *How is it parted?*

Q: *How high is his forehead?*

Q: *Is his hair thick or thin?*

Q: *Is it straight, curly, wavy or kinky?*

Q: *Does he have a mustache? A beard?*

Q: *What color are his eyes?*

Q: *Are his eyebrows thick and bushy, or thin?*

Q: *Is his mouth large or small?*

Q: *Does he wear glasses?*

Q: *Does he have any gold teeth? Braces?*

Q: *Is his nose large or small, straight or curved?*

Q: *Does he have any facial scars?*

Q: *Any visible tatoos?*

Q: *Any apparent deformities?*

Q: *Is he stocky, thin, or medium?*

Q: *Broadshouldered or narrow shouldered?*

Q: *Are his earlobes attached at the bottom or curved upward?*

If you commit yourself to an answer to every one of these questions, the odds are <u>against</u> your getting them all right. Some cops are observant enough and have a good enough memory to do it, and if you really can, go ahead—it's devastating to the defense when the guy comes out and fits your description in every detail!

But most cops can't do that. Don't be ashamed if you can't; even a very good cop sees far too many people between arrest and trial to recall all those physical characteristics perfectly. So if you don't really know the answer to any (or all) of those questions, DON'T GUESS — just say: "I don't know," or "I couldn't tell you that now," or something like that. Because *you* know who's going to get devastated if you take a bunch of wild guesses and the guy who walks out is different in half a dozen or more respects from what you described.

Also, bear in mind that some things—especially hair styles and facial hair—are easily and often changed between arrest and trial. So if questions are put to you about how the defendant looks *now,* and you haven't seen him for awhile, be sure to say so:

Q: *How long is his hair?*
A: *I have no way of knowing how long it is now.*

Don't worry if the defense attorney asks you *all* of the questions listed above and you have to say "I don't know" to *all* or *most* of them. Either you or the prosecutor is going to get a chance to point out to the jury that your inability to answer these questions doesn't affect your ability to make a positive identification when you see the defendant. If the defense attorney gives *you* the chance, here's one way to handle it:

A: *I couldn't tell you.*

Q: *Well, Officer, if you can't tell me about any of those obvious physical features that I've just asked you about, I take it you would be unable to identify the person we've been discussing. Is that right?*

A: *No, sir. That's not right at all.*

Q: *You mean you think you could identify him?*

A: *I'm sure I can.*

Q: *How is it possible, Officer, that you can <u>identify</u> someone you don't seem to be able to <u>describe</u> very well?*

A: *It's possible because unless some permanent, striking feature stands out, I notice people as a <u>whole</u>, not by the thickness of their eyebrows or the length of their nose. And when I see them again, I recognize them from their <u>total</u> features—not from one or two isolated things. I can't tell you which type of earlobes Johnny Carson has, but if he comes into this courtroom, I can point him out for you. And I can do the same with this defendant.*

IT TAKES TWO TO TANGLE

It's true that lawyers have a lot of control in the courtroom. But there are a few things <u>you</u> have control over, too. One of them is how fast you let the defense attorney fire questions at you. He can talk as fast as he wants to, but he can't ask the next question until <u>you've</u> <u>answered</u> the last one. So just because *he's* trying to keep things going so rapid-fire that he gets you too wound up to think straight doesn't mean *you* have to play along. When you see that he's trying to put you on a roller coaster, just pause a little longer before answering, and deliberately slow down your own tempo as you reply. He can't run a rapid cross-examination all by himself.

The defense attorney may try to control the impression your testimony makes by controlling your voice. People tend to imitate. So if the examiner raises or lowers his voice, the witness tends to do the same. If you see that the attorney is consciously changing his own volume or speed or inflection, don't go along with him. Maintain an audible voice, even if he's whispering his questions. And keep your tone the same, even if he starts shouting. Once he realizes he doesn't have control over your reactions, he'll probably stop screwing around.

DON'T ANSWER NON-QUESTIONS

Sometimes the defense attorney makes a statement that isn't a question at all, and then he pauses just to see if you volunteer some reaction. Don't.

EXAMPLE

Non-Q: *Well, Officer, that seems a little hard to believe.*

(You may be tempted to say: "Maybe so, but that's exactly what happened." Don't do it. You haven't been asked anything—just sit there and wait for a question.)

If the defense attorney throws out a non-question and everyone in the courtroom keeps looking at you as if they expect you to say something, say this:

A: *If that was a question, sir, I don't understand what the question is.*

That puts the monkey on his back to formulate a question or get on to something else.

DON'T BE IMPRESSED

Defense attorneys are on an ego trip about 75% of the time. They like to show off to the jury, and they like to try to show you *up* in front of the jury. One way they try to do that is by asking a technical question that you don't know the answer to. They hope that your own ego will force you to make some kind of guess, just so you aren't outdone in your own field by a smart-aleck lawyer. Guesses always help the defense.

EXAMPLE

Q: *Officer, you know what the term "lateral nystagmus" means, don't you?*

A: *Uh . . . yes.*

Q: *What does it mean?*

A: *Uh . . . well . . . that has to do with the movement of the eyes.*

Q: *Yes, but specifically what does it mean?*

A: *Uh . . . that's a term that's used when you're . . . uh . . . describing the movement of the eyes . . .*

> *uh . . . the eyes of someone who is . . . uh . . .*
> *who may be under the influence of opiates.*
> **Q:** *Yes, but when you use that term, exactly what*
> *does it mean?*
> **A:** *Well, I'm not . . . uh . . . 100% sure what it*
> *means exactly, but I've . . . uh . . . heard it used*
> *a lot.*

You just look foolish trying to kid people. If you don't know what something means—even if you think you should—don't beat around the bush; just say you aren't sure what it means.

Another defense tactic is to try to embarrass you with a lot of unfamiliar vocabulary. Don't be embarrassed. Here's your chance to make points with the jury—*they* don't know what all the attorney's technical terms and law-school vocabulary mean, either. They'll make a hero out of you if you *say* what they're *thinking:*

> **Q:** *Officer, as a condition precedent to your puncti-*
> *lious courtroom performance, was your antici-*
> *pated testimony a product of controlled ingemi-*
> *nation, with the prosecutor here as preceptor?*

If you have a little theatrical talent and seem to be standing in good stead with the judge and jury so far, you might have a little fun with something like that. Maybe you pause for a couple of seconds, look over at the jury with a quizzical expression on your face, look back to the attorney, pause a little longer, smile broadly and say: "Could you say all that again?"

Otherwise, just say: "I don't understand that question at all." Make him put it into understandable English (and keep all your answers in everyday English), and the jury will love you for it.

LIVING WITH YOUR REPORT

This topic is covered exhaustively in my report writing manual, and the following examples are taken from that book. If you've already read it, skip over to the next topic.

Defense attorneys like to be able to take something significant from your <u>testimony</u>, make you admit that it wasn't even mentioned in your <u>report</u>, and then suggest to you that since you wrote the <u>report</u> while everything was fresher in your memory than it is now, you must be mistaken in your testimony. I've seen cop after cop *help* the defense attorney pull this stunt by allowing the attorney to put words in their mouth, like this:

Q: *Now, Officer, you wrote a report about this arrest, didn't you?*

A: *Yes, sir.*

Q: *And wasn't the purpose of that report to record all the important information about the case?*

A: *Yes, I guess so.*

Q: *I take it, Officer, that these events were clearer in your mind when you wrote the report than they are now, some six months later, right?*

Whether you write your report in the field . . .

. . . or in the station, be sure it's a report you can
<u>live</u> <u>with</u> in court.

A: *That's right.*

Q: *Did you deliberately leave out any significant details when you wrote the report?*

A: *No, sir.*

Q: *Don't you think it's significant to know which one of these men hit the other one first?*

A: *Yes.*

Q: *And it's your testimony today that you saw Sharp hit Peters first, is that right?*

A: *That's right.*

Q: *Now Officer, did you put that in your report?*

A: *No, I guess I didn't.*

Q: *Would you care to explain to the jury, Officer, whether you left that out of your report because you didn't consider it significant at the time, or whether it's something you've just now re-called, six months later?*

There's no good way to get out of this, once you've gotten yourself into it. The solution is to *refuse* to let the defense attorney sell you on some of those mistaken premises—don't let him make up your answers for you.

Q: *Now, Officer, you wrote a report about this arrest, didn't you?*

A: *Yes, sir.*

Q: *And wasn't the purpose of that report to record all the important information about this case?*

A: *Not exactly. It's hardly ever possible to record <u>all</u> the information, so my report is usually more* like a summary than a complete account of every single thing.

Q: But you do try to include in your report all the important details, don't you?

A: If I can tell at the time which details are going to prove to _be_ important, yes sir. I can't always foresee what will turn out to be important in every case.

Q: I take it, Officer, that these events were clearer in your mind when you wrote the report than they are now, some six months later, right?

A: _Some_ of them were, naturally, but some things are just as clear in my mind now as they ever were.

Q: Did you deliberately leave out any significant details when you wrote the report?

A: Not _deliberately_, but _necessarily_. Since I can't possibly put down everything, or anticipate what others will consider to be "significant," I do my best to give an accurate summary of what happened.

Q: Don't you think it's significant to know which one of these men hit the other one first?

A: Yes.

Q: And it's your testimony today that you saw Sharp hit Peters first, is that right?

A: That's right.

Q: Now, Officer, did you put that in your report?

A: No, I didn't.

Q: Would you care to explain to the jury, Officer,

whether you left that out of your report because you didn't consider it significant at the time, or whether it's something you've just now recalled, six months later?

A: *I'd be glad to explain it. I've been on the witness stand testifying about this for an hour and twenty minutes. I wrote my report in fifteen minutes. If I could afford to spend as much time writing each report as I spend testifying, I suppose I could include as many details, but I can't do that, or I wouldn't get any police work done. So I try to make every report a fair and accurate summary, and in doing that, I realize there are going to be times when something will be left out that may turn out later to be significant. Usually, if it's that significant, it will stand out in my memory, the way it does now that I saw Sharp hit Peters first.*

NO RHYME OR REASON

The defense attorney may pick out something you did at the arrest scene, or something you did not do, and try to make it look like you don't know *why* you do the things you do:

Q: *Now, in your testimony here, you've said the defendant swayed about 6 inches in each direction. In your report, you just say he swayed, but don't mention how far. Is there any reason why you didn't put the 6 inches in your report?*

A: *No, sir.*

Q: *You sometimes use the alphabet test, don't you?*

A: *Yes, sir.*

Q: *Is there any reason why you didn't offer that test to Mr. Clark here?*

A: *No, sir.*

Q: *By the way, did Mr. Clark have any containers of liquor in his car when you stopped him?*

A: *No, sir.*

Q: *Is there any particular reason why you didn't mention that in your direct testimony earlier?*

A: *No, sir.*

Every single answer this cop gave to the "is there any reason" questions was <u>wrong</u>! He has allowed the defense attorney to make it look as if he just does things, and omits things, without any rhyme or reason. And that's simply not the case:

Q: *. . . Is there any reason why you didn't put the 6 inches in your report?*

A: *Yes, sir.*

Q: *What is the reason?*

A: *I can't sit there writing all night, trying to include every possible detail I can think of. In fact, I can't afford to spend more than a fraction of the time writing a report that I spend testifying about it in court. If I did that, I'd probably only be able to handle about one*

> *case a day. I have to leave some things out, so there's probably <u>always</u> going to be some things in my testimony that aren't in my report.*

Q: *... Is there any reason why you didn't offer the alphabet test to Mr. Clark?*

A: *Yes, sir.*

Q: *Why is that?*

A: *I have to stop at some point—I can't just stand out there all night giving every test I can think of. After Mr. Clark had failed all five of the tests I'd given him, I didn't see any purpose in running him through more and more tests.*

Q: *By the way, did Mr. Clark have any containers of liquor in his car when you stopped him?*

A: *No, sir.*

Q: *Is there any particular reason why you didn't mention that in your direct testimony earlier?*

A: *Yes, sir.*

Q: *Why?*

A: *Because I wasn't asked about it.*

<u>Everything</u> you do or fail to do has a reason. Maybe the reason is just that it wasn't necessary, or it didn't occur to you, or you didn't have a chance to do it, or you simply forgot. If those are the reasons, own up to it. But don't let yourself sound like a haphazard bungler. Don't tell the jury that there's no reason for the way you do your job.

WHAT'S SO INCREDIBLE?

We talked about the "eyepatch" bluff. Another tactic to try to shake your self-confidence is for the defense attorney to act completely startled at some answer you've given, and then to repeat your answer back to you as a question, emphasizing one of your words or phrases as if he finds that absolutely incredible. Just this simple little trick sends some witnesses backing up the road, suddenly (and unnecessarily) unsure of their own testimony:

Q: *What did he do then?*

A: *He grabbed the handle of my service revolver and started pulling it up out of the holster.*

Q: *With three other armed officers standing right there, he grabbed your gun and started pulling it out of your holster?*

A: *Well, he . . . everything was pretty confused and all happened so quick . . .*

You see? Backing down just because the defense attorney sounded like he found it hard to believe. If you know what you're talking about, don't let the defense attorney start you to doubting:

Q: *With three other armed officers standing right there, he grabbed your gun and started pulling it out of your holster?*

A: *Yes, sir. That's what he did.*

DON'T APOLOGIZE FOR DOING YOUR JOB

The defense lawyer may try to make you look like a bully or a Gestapo agent just for doing your job. He's most likely to try that in cases where you had to use some kind of force on the defendant. Don't try to minimize what the defendant forced you to do. If you say you just tapped him, and the hospital records show he had multiple fractures and bruises when you brought him in, your credibility isn't worth the price of a free donut.

One of my idols when I was a cop was a guy named Byron Pompeo. He was always farthest from the call and always the first one to get there. Byron never suffered from a lack of self-confidence; he always seemed to know exactly what he was doing, and he could put the kind of command in his voice that got instant respect from most people.

But once in awhile, someone would try Byron on for size (although he was built like a fire plug, he wasn't that tall, as cops go). It was always a mistake for some challenger to get tough with him, and if the case went to trial, use of force always popped up as an issue. But Byron was always able to justify his reactions, and he never apologized for doing whatever was necessary to control a cop-fighter. His answers on the stand weren't defensive or arrogant—just matter-of-fact. It usually went like this:

Q: *What happened next?*

A: *He doubled up his fist and swung it right through the space where my head would have been if I hadn't ducked.*

Q: *Then what did you do?*

A: *I hit him in the face with my fist.*

Q: *Oh! After he* missed *you, you* hit *him in the face with your fist! And how hard did you hit him, Officer Pompeo?*

A: *Just as hard as I could.*

It should go without saying, but just to keep your insurance carrier happy, I'll remind you that you've got to conduct yourself at all times in the field in such a way that you'll have nothing to apologize *for*. That means staying within legal and departmental limits on use of force, and being absolutely certain that you can justify every move you make. If you've done that, you don't owe anybody any apologies. So don't start sounding sorry on the witness stand.

You can regret *having* to use force (you certainly don't want to sound *proud* of it); but if the defendant made your use of force necessary, you don't need to regret meeting the requirements of your job. If the only reasonable way to deal with the defendant's violence was with a decisive use of force, don't let the defense attorney make it look like you've got something to be ashamed of.

DON'T MAKE ME SICK

I once tried a child abandonment case where the pivotal witness was a detective who had been a cop for eight years. I guess he was the single worst witness I've ever seen—cop or civilian. He did everything wrong (needless to say, we lost a perfectly good case). That wasn't the first case I ever watched go down the tubes because of an unprepared, unconvincing witness. It wasn't the last.

But it was the most <u>disgusting</u> in one respect: after the detective had been on the stand for a couple of hours of cross-examination and had let the defense attorney make a sweaty, nervous, hand-trembling shambles out of him, this eight-year veteran walked up to the defense attorney in the hallway during recess. He gave the attorney a nervous grin, shook his hand, patted his shoulder, and said: "Counsel, I want to congratulate you . . . that was a great job of cross-examination! No hard feelings, huh? Good work!"

I couldn't believe it! The whole revolting scene was enough to turn your stomach. The jurors who were walking down the hallway didn't bother hiding the contempt in their faces, either. It's one thing to let a clever lawyer get the best of you in the court-room. But it's something else to run after him in the hallway after he's done it and kiss him for it. If your prosecutor ever sees you do something like that, I hope he'll tell you the same thing I told my detective: "You're in the wrong line of work, buster. Why don't you get the hell out so they can put a real cop in your slot?"

I've advised you throughout this book to remain respectful and courteous to the attorneys, even if they're not. But that doesn't mean you should overdo it and fall in love with them.

PROTECT YOURSELF

Part of the judge's job is to keep witnesses from being browbeaten by the attorneys. I think about 99% of the judges will do a pretty fair job of it. And when you're being cross-examined, it's part of the prosecutor's job to keep you from being subjected to improper questioning. Most prosecutors won't let you down.

But there may be times when you'll bump into an inexperienced prosecutor who feels intimidated by a more experienced defense lawyer, or a prosecutor who's just plain weak, lazy, unknowledgeable or indifferent. If you find yourself in that situation, you may have to be a little more self-protective than usual. So here's a couple more booby traps to watch out for.

1. If the lawyer asks you a compound question, don't try to give a single answer. **A compound question** simply means there's two or more separate questions asked together.

EXAMPLE

Q: *Officer, did you yourself take that packet out of the glove compartment, or did you see any other officer, or anyone else present, take that packet out of the glove compartment and dispose of it?*

There are four questions in one. Whether you answer "yes" or "no," it won't be clear whether you're answering about your taking it out, or another officer, or someone else taking it, and it won't be clear whether you know who took it but don't know how they disposed of it.

If your prosecutor fails to object to a compound question, protect yourself:

A: *I don't understand which of those things you're asking me.*

Q: *I'm asking you all of them.*

A: *What was the first question, please?*

Or, if you can recall the entire question, you can handle it this way:

A: *Now, let's see . . . I did not take it out myself. I did not see another officer take it out. Yes, I did see the defendant's wife take it out, and no, I didn't see her dispose of it.*

2. If the lawyer misquotes your earlier testimony or assumes as a fact something that you don't know to *be* a fact, don't try to answer the question. If the prosecutor fails to object, protect yourself:

Q: *Well, you say he was falling all over the place— was he asking you for help?*

A: *I didn't say he was falling all over the place—I*

said he was <u>stumbling</u> all over the place. No, he didn't ask for help.

Q: *Were you still choking him around the neck when he begged you to stop hurting him?*

(If you were *never* choking him around the neck, and if he *never* begged you to stop hurting him, this question assumes two facts that you're not willing to accept. But even if you answer "no," it still sounds like these two things *happened,* just not at the same time.)

A: *I don't know what you're talking about . . . there was never a time when I was choking him, and there was never a time when he said anything about being hurt.*

Now remember, these are only appropriate responses if your prosecutor isn't making the necessary objections. In most cases, he'll be alert and jumping up and down if the defense lawyer pulls any of these things, so you won't have to worry about it.

Okay. Now, you're informed. At this point in the book, you're better-informed than most of the millions of witnesses who have climbed into the witness chairs in millions of trials before you. That shouldn't make you feel like an expert, but it should give you the confidence to do several hundred percent better at handling cross-examination the next time you testify.

My earlier precaution is a continuing one: it's not possible for me to anticipate or cover every different ploy a cross-examiner can take. But by now you should have a good enough insight into the proper <u>approach</u> that you'll be able to handle whatever pops up. Just keep cool, use your judgment, and don't get in a hurry.

□

QUALIFYING AS AN EXPERT

Most cops won't need most of the material in this chapter. But most of you will need some of it, sometime (so don't throw the book away after you finish reading it).

A person who has special knowledge, skill, or experience in any occupation, trade or craft may be qualified as an expert witness in his field. Common examples of expert witnesses are pathologists, psychiatrists, physicists, chemists and engineers. Police officers who concentrate on a particular phase of police work should eventually qualify as an expert witness in that area of concentration.

So what if you're an expert? That allows you to give an **expert opinion** in court—and the jury can rely on it as such—in the area of your expertise. Sometimes it's hard to prove something any other way except through an expert opinion. For instance, if the burglar leaves fingerprints all over the crime scene, and you have his exemplars on file, it's easy enough to get both sets of prints introduced against the guy in court. But a jury can't look at them and tell they were both made by the same person. So how do we prove they were? With the *opinion* of a fingerprint examiner.

If you find yourself working one particular assignment for an extended period of time, whether it's traffic accidents, narcotics, checks, bookmaking, auto theft, or crime lab, you're going to acquire a lot of specialized knowledge. And the time is going to come when the prosecutor will need to put you on the stand and try to prove you're sufficiently qualified to give an expert opinion.

Procedurally, the questions will follow this sequence: your identification and employment; your background and qualifications in your field of expertise; then either a hypothetical question based on facts that have been proved in the trial, or questions to establish that you personally examined the questioned evidence; and finally, your opinion as to the hypothetical question or the examined evidence.

After the prosecutor has finished his questions about your qualifications, and *before* he gets into the facts of this case with you, the defense attorney has the opportunity to ask further questions about your expertise, and to object to your giving an opinion, if he doesn't think you're really an expert. During all of this questioning by both sides, you should follow the guidelines we've already discussed.

To help you prepare yourself for the kinds of questions you can expect during the qualifying phase, here are typical lists of questions in three of the most commonly-used expert fields.

USE OF NARCOTICS

Q: *Officer, by whom are you employed?*

Q: *In what capacity?*

Q: *How long have you been so employed?*

Q: *Have you had previous employment in a similar capacity?*

Q: *When and where?*

Q: *Have you received any special academic training in the field of narcotics law enforcement?*

Q: *Please describe when and where that training occurred, and what it covered?*

Q: *Have you also received specialized training within your department in the enforcement of narcotics laws?*

Q: *Please describe that training.*

Q: *Have you taken any related courses at any college, university, or technical training centers?*

Q: *Please describe that training.*

Q: *Have you read any publications that dealt with the subject of narcotics usage?*

Q: *Please describe.*

Q: *Have you written any publications on the subject?*

Q: *Please describe.*

Q: *Have you done any teaching on the subject?*

Q: *Do you have any other special training in this field?*

Q: *Please describe.*

Q: *Was _____ one of the narcotic substances covered by your training?*

Q: *Were you trained in the recognition of _____ as you might expect to encounter it in your duties?*

Q: *What characteristics were you trained to look for in the recognition of _____ ?*

Q: *Does _____ exist as a powder, a liquid, a capsule or a tablet?*

Q: *What, if anything, is distinctive about its color?*

Q: *What is distinctive about its shape?*

Q: *What is distinctive about its odor?*

Q: *What is distinctive about its size?*

Q: *What is distinctive about its texture?*

Q: *Are there any other identifying peculiarities?*

Q: *Are there any tests that can be performed on _____ to confirm its identity?*

Q: *How many that you know of?*

Q: *What are they?*

Q: *Have you ever performed any of these tests yourself?*

Q: *Which ones?*

Q: *How many times?*

Q: *How did you learn to do that?*

Q: *What procedure do you follow?*

Q: *What do the results tell you?*

Q: *How?*

Q: *Are these tests conclusive?*

Q: *Have you been able to obtain independent confirmation of your test results?*

Q: *How?*

Q: *In what percentage of these cases were your own results confirmed?*

Q: *Did any of your training describe common methods by which _____ is used, other than by medical personnel?*

Q: *What are they?*

Q: *Have you found that _____ is normally packaged in a particular manner, other than by medical personnel?*

Q: *How?*

Q: *Have you had on-the-job experience enforcing narcotics laws?*

Q: *For how long?*

Q: *How many cases have you investigated?*

Q: *Did your training cover physical symptoms that you would expect to observe in a person who had used or was under the influence of _____ ?*

Q: *Please describe those symptoms and the time intervals at which you would expect them to be observable.*

Q: *Have you observed such symptoms in any suspected _____ users you have observed in your experience?*

Q: *In what percentage of them?*

Q: *Are there any physical or chemical tests which tend to confirm that a person has or has not used _____ ?*

Q: *What are they?*

Q: *Can you perform any of these tests yourself?*

Q: *Which ones?*

Q: *How did you learn them?*

Q: *What procedure do you follow?*

Q: *How many times have you performed that kind of test?*

Q: *What result tends to indicate that the tested person has used or is under the influence of _____ ?*

Q: *What kind of result tends to indicate in the negative?*

Q: *Are these tests conclusive?*

Q: *Can these tests be confirmed by any kind of laboratory or chemical test?*

Q: *What is it?*

Q: *Is this test conclusive?*

Q: *How many times have you examined what you recognized as _____?*

Q: *Have you sought laboratory analysis in any of those cases?*

Q: *What percentage?*

Q: *In what percentage of those submitted samples was your own opinion confirmed by analysis?*

Q: *How many suspected _____ users have you examined?*

Q: *Have you performed or sought chemical tests on any of those suspects?*

Q: *How many?*

Q: *In what percentage of these cases were your*

opinions confirmed?

Q: *Are there any particular devices or materials that are normally used by someone to (inject) (smoke) (ingest) _____ ?*

Q: *What are they?*

Q: *What is the purpose of each of these items?*

Q: *Have you previously qualified as an expert witness in the field of narcotics use and influence?*

Q: *How many times?*

Q: *Did you examine the substance in this package, Exhibit 4?*

Q: *How do you know?*

Q: *When did you do that?*

Q: *Where?*

Q: *Describe your examination.*

Q: *Did you recognize any qualities of this substance which are characteristic of any particular narcotic?*

Q: *What are they?*

Q: *Do you have an opinion as to what this substance is?*

Q: *What is that opinion?*

Q: *Did you perform an evaluation of the defendant for possible use or influence of _____ on September 5, 1979?*

Q: *Where?*

Q: *Please describe your evaluation.*

Q: *Did you notice any symptoms which are characteristically displayed by one who has used or is under the influence of _____ ?*

Q: *What were they?*

Q: *Do you have an opinion as to whether the defendant had used or was under the influence of _____ at the time you examined him?*

Q: *What is that opinion?*

The prosecutor will tailor his questions to your case and your personal qualifications. Be sure to let him know if it would be pointless of him to ask you any particular question (such as whether or not you've written any publications).

FINGERPRINT COMPARISONS

Q: *Officer, by whom are you employed?*

Q: *In what capacity?*

Q: *How long have you been so employed?*

Q: *Have you had prior law enforcement experience?*

Q: *When and where?*

Q: *Have you had any special training in the science of fingerprints?*

Q: *Please describe when and where that training occurred, and what it covered.*

Q: *Have you also received on-the-job experience in taking and comparing fingerprints?*

Q: *Please describe the nature and extent of that experience.*

Q: *Have you taken any academic courses at college or training institutions where fingerprint science was covered?*

Q: *Please describe the training, including the dates and locations of the various courses.*

Q: *Have you read any publications on the subject?*

Q: *Please detail those.*

Q: *Do you subscribe to or regularly read any periodicals on the subject of fingerprints?*

Q: *Do you belong to any professional organizations relating to fingerprint science?*

Q: *What are they?*

Q: *What are their purposes and activities?*

Q: *Have you taught any classes on the subject of fingerprints?*

Q: *When and where?*

Q: *Do you have any other special training or experience in this field that we haven't covered?*

Q: *Please describe.*

Q: *Would you please explain to the jury what is meant by the term "latent" fingerprint?*

Q: *Has your own training and experience included lifting latent prints?*

Q: *Approximately how many times have you lifted latent prints?*

Q: *Is there more than one way to develop latents?*

Q: *Would you please explain briefly how each of these methods works?*

Q: *Have you used all of these various methods?*

Q: *How are the developed latents preserved?*

Q: *What kinds of conditions at the crime scene can affect your ability to develop and use latents?*

Q: *Does the passage of time affect your ability to*

develop latents?

Q: *Explain.*

Q: *Could conditions of the suspect's hands or foreign substances on his hands affect your ability to develop workable latents?*

Q: *Explain.*

Q: *Are there such things as usable prints of any parts of the hand other than the finger and thumb prints?*

Q: *Please explain.*

Q: *What is an "ink impression?"*

Q: *How are these obtained?*

Q: *Have you been trained in the proper procedure for obtaining ink-impression exemplars?*

Q: *What procedure do you follow?*

Q: *Approximately how many times have you rolled ink impressions?*

Q: *Once you have obtained latent prints from the crime scene, and ink impressions from a known suspect, is there a comparison procedure which permits a trained and experienced fingerprint analyst to draw conclusions as to how well the latents do, or do not, compare with the ink exemplars?*

Q: *Have you been trained in making such comparisons?*

Q: *Approximately how many such comparisons have you made?*

Q: *Have any of your comparisons been subject to independent verification, such as through con-*

firmation by another analyst, or corroboration by confessions or other physical evidence, or through controlled experiments, so that your opinions could be checked for accuracy?

Q: *In what approximate percentage of your cases have you had such an opportunity for verification?*

Q: *Of those, in what approximate percentage of cases were your opinions confirmed as correct?*

Q: *Basically, how does the comparison procedure work?*

Q: *Is it normal practice to roll ink impressions of victims and others who may lawfully have left latent prints at the crime scene?*

Q: *Why is this done?*

Q: *After you have eliminated those latents which match the prints of victims and other non-suspects, do you then conduct an evaluation of the remaining latents, if any, in comparison with a suspect's rolled prints?*

Q: *Is there a standard system of classifying fingerprints according to recurring types?*

Q: *How many types are there?*

Q: *Would you please sketch for the jury an example of these various features, labelling each one by name?*

Q: *What are "ridge characteristics?"*

Q: *Please sketch examples of the various characteristics that you look for in fingerprints, and label each.*

Q: *Of all the features you've sketched, which of them can be used for comparison purposes in order to identify fingerprints?*

Q: *Is there any standard number of similarities that are required before an analyst can conclude that there is a match?*

Q: *What number of similarities do you usually require to satisfy yourself that you do indeed have a match?*

Q: *In your opinion, is it possible for latent prints and inked impressions to have _____ points of similarity and not be the prints of one and the same person?*

Q: *Have you previously qualified in court before as an expert witness on the subject of fingerprint comparisons?*

Q: *How many times?*

Q: *I show you this (latent) card marked for identification as people's exhibit 12—do you recognize this?*

Q: *What is it?*

Q: *How do you know?*

Q: *Did you lift and transfer to this card the latents preserved here?*

Q: *When and where?*

Q: *In doing that, did you follow the normal procedure, which you previously described?*

Q: *Where did you place the cards after that?*

Q: *When did you next see this card?*

Q: *I now show you this (exemplar) card, marked*

for identification as people's 13—do you recognize this?

Q: What is it?

Q: Did you roll these impressions yourself?

Q: Were they taken from the defendant, the man seated at the far end of the table there?

Q: On what date?

Q: Did you follow the normal procedure for rolling impressions, as you explained it earlier?

Q: This photographic display is numbered for identification as people's 14—do you recognize it?

Q: What is it?

Q: Did you make it yourself?

Q: When?

Q: For what purpose?

Q: Have you examined the prints depicted on this display, both photographically and directly, with magnification of the prints themselves?

Q: Do the photographs on the display correctly depict the points themselves, except for the fact that all features are proportionately larger due to the enlargement of the photos?

Q: Have you conducted a comparison of the latent prints found at the crime scene with the ink impressions which you took from the defendant?

Q: Did you find any points of similarity?

Q: How many?

Q: Would you please point them out for the jury,

> *labelling them with letters of the alphabet as you go, and using the same letter on each part of the display to indicate corresponding parts— in other words, an "A" on each photo to indicate the first similar point, and so on.*
>
> **Q:** *What is it about each of these features that you found to be similar?*
>
> **Q:** *Did you find any dissimilarities in your analysis which would indicate that these prints were not made by one and the same person?*
>
> **Q:** *Do you feel that it's possible to form an opinion from the number of similarities you found, as to whether or not the latent prints lifted at the crime scene were made by the same person whose inked impressions you have identified here as being the defendant's?*
>
> **Q:** *Do you have such an opinion?*
>
> **Q:** *What is it?*
>
> **Q:** *In your opinion, is it possible that any other person in the world besides the defendant left those particular latents at the crime scene?*

If you weren't the one who lifted the latents, or rolled the exemplar, some other witness will have testified to those things before you get called, and many of these questions will have been asked of him, and won't be asked of you.

If you can't define and sketch arches, whorls, loops, cores, deltas, bifurcations, islands, dots, and abrupt ending ridges, don't get up to testify as an expert on comparisons. If you lifted the latents, be sure you can explain in basic terms the difference between dusting, iodine fumes, silver-nitrate solutions, and micro-photography. Be especially well-versed on the procedure you actually used in the case at trial.

TRAFFIC ACCIDENT RECONSTRUCTION

Q: *By whom are you employed, Officer?*

Q: *In what capacity?*

Q: *How long have you been employed by_____?*

Q: *How long have you worked as an accident investigator?*

Q: *Did you have prior law enforcement experience?*

Q: *Where and when?*

Q: *Did those duties also involve accident investigation?*

Q: *Have you had any special classroom training in accident investigation?*

Q: *Please describe that training.*

Q: *Have you had supervised, on-the-job training in accident investigation?*

Q: *Please describe that.*

Q: *Approximately how many traffic accidents have you investigated?*

Q: *Have you read any publications on the topic of accident investigation?*

Q: *Please describe.*

Q: *Do you subscribe to any periodicals which report on accident investigation topics?*

Q: *Which ones?*

Q: *Have you written any publications on the subject?*

Q: *Please describe them.*

Q: *Have you observed any controlled-crash experiments?*

Q: *Please describe those, including when and where they occurred.*

Q: *Have you read reports of controlled-crash experiments?*

Q: *Please describe those.*

Q: *What is a "skid pan?"*

Q: *Have you conducted or observed any "skid pan" demonstrations?*

Q: *Please describe those.*

Q: *Have you conducted or observed any emergency-stop demonstrations?*

Q: *Please describe.*

Q: *Have you observed any other traffic experiments?*

Q: *Please describe those.*

Q: *Have you taught any classes on accident investigation?*

Q: *Please describe.*

Q: *Have you trained other officers in the investigation of accidents?*

Q: *How many?*

Q: *What is meant by "accident reconstruction?"*

Q: *How many methods of "accident reconstruction" are you familiar with?*

Q: *What are they?*

Q: *Basically, how does each work?*

Q: *If a person driving down the street perceives a danger of collision ahead of him, how many alternatives for avoiding it does he usually have to consider?*

Q: *Is there a fairly standard time that it takes most people to decide whether to do nothing, speed up, brake, or turn, to avoid a collision, and then to begin to react accordingly?*

Q: *What is that amount of time for most people?*

Q: *Is there a formula for converting speeds of miles per hour into feet per second?*

Q: *What is that formula?*

Q: *Using that formula, would you please make a chart on the blackboard, showing the feet-per-second equivalent of the following mile-per-hour values: 20, 30, 40, 50, 60 and 70?*

Q: *Assuming the standard reaction time of .75 seconds, would you please add to the chart a column showing the distance, in feet, that a vehicle would travel during reaction time at those various speeds?*

Q: *Is there a difference in meaning between the terms "speed" or "velocity," and "acceleration?"*

Q: *Would you please define those terms for the jury and explain the difference?*

Q: *What are "skidmarks?"*

Q: *What causes a vehicle to leave skidmarks?*

Q: Do the skidmarks begin at the moment the brakes are applied?

Q: Is there a method for determining how far a vehicle would travel in the lag period between the time when the brakes are applied and the time when they locked and began leaving skidmarks?

Q: Please explain.

Q: What method is used to measure skidmarks?

Q: How do you insure accuracy in your measurements?

Q: How can you determine which of the wheels on a vehicle left which of the skids?

Q: Can a reliable estimate of a vehicle's speed be determined from a measurement of skids?

Q: Is there a standard formula for this relationship?

Q: What is it?

Q: Would you please define and explain "coefficient of friction?"

Q: Can that be measured?

Q: How do you do that?

Q: How is the coefficient of friction expressed?

Q: Could other variable factors affect the computation of speed from skids?

Q: What would be the effect, if any, of type of road surface?

Q: What effect from ice, snow, water, oil, sand, or gravel, for example, on the roadway?

Q: What about dilapidation of the road?

Q: What effect of road temperature differences?

Q: *How about the temperature of the tires?*

Q: *What effect from the type of tire, and its tread design and depth?*

Q: *What about tire inflation?*

Q: *What about braking efficiency?*

Q: *Would you define the terms "slope" and "grade?"*

Q: *How would those affect your computations?*

Q: *Would there be any effect based on type and weight of the vehicle?*

Q: *Please explain.*

Q: *What about weather conditions, including wind?*

Q: *Is there any standard "tolerance" value used in your computations to allow for the range of variance in those conditions which you can't measure after an accident has occurred?*

Q: *Please explain.*

Q: *Do you take into account the energy used in a collision?*

Q: *How is that determined?*

Q: *What is a "foot-pound?"*

Q: *Please describe your experience in determining expended energy in traffic collisions.*

Q: *Are there any other factors affecting the speed-skid ratio?*

Q: *Please explain.*

Q: *What is "critical speed?"*

Q: *What happens if the critical speed is exceeded?*

Q: *What is a "centrifugal skid?"*

Q: *What might cause scuff marks on the roadway?*

Q: *What might cause scratches?*

Q: *What might cause gouges in the road?*

Q: *How is point of impact determined?*

Q: *What is a "paint transfer?"*

Q: *What can you tell from a paint transfer?*

Q: *What can you tell from the location, nature, and extent of damage to the vehicles?*

Q: *Please explain.*

Q: *What can you tell from the nature and extent of injuries to occupants of the vehicles?*

Q: *Please explain.*

Q: *What can you tell from damage to objects such as poles, trees, fences and shrubs?*

Q: *Please explain.*

Q: *Have you previously qualified in court as an expert witness on the subject of traffic accident reconstruction?*

Q: *How many times?*

Q: *How many times have you performed accident reconstruction studies?*

Q: *Did you investigate a traffic accident which occurred on June 19, 1979, about 10:30 p.m. at the intersection of 18th and Vincent in the City of Orange?*

Q: *What time did you arrive?*

Q: *Did you notice any damaged vehicles within the intersection when you arrived?*

Q: *Were there any indications to you that those vehicles had just been involved in a collision somewhere within that intersection?*

Q: *What were these indications?*

Q: *Were you able to establish a point of impact?*

Q: *How?*

Q: *Where was it?*

Q: *Were you able to determine the original direction of travel of each vehicle?*

Q: *How?*

Q: *What was it?*

Q: *Did you measure the street and lane widths?*

Q: *How?*

Q: *What were they? (Probably use a diagram.)*

Q: *Were there any traffic controls at that intersection?*

Q: *Please describe them.*

Q: *Did you examine them that evening during the course of your investigation?*

Q: *Were they working properly?*

Q: *How could you tell?*

Q: *Were they obscured by anything that you noticed?*

Q: *Were the lanes clearly marked?*

Q: *How?*

Q: *Were there marked crosswalks or stop limit lines?*

Q: *Where?*

Q: *How were they designated?*

Q: *What kind of street surface is each street there?*

Q: *Is either street curved within _____ feet of the intersection?*

Q: *Does either street have a measureable slope or grade within _____ feet of the intersection?*

Q: *Which?*

Q: *Where?*

Q: *Have you measured it?*

Q: *How?*

Q: *What measurement did you obtain?*

Q: *Were you able to determine the coefficient of friction of each street within _____ feet of the intersection?*

Q: *How?*

Q: *What values did you obtain?*

Q: *Did you examine the roadway of both streets?*

Q: *Did you find on either any of the conditions you previously listed which might appreciably affect skidmark speed computations?*

Q: *Where?*

Q: *What were they?*

Q: *Did you notice the weather conditions?*

Q: *Were there any conditions that would have affected skidmark speed computations?*

Q: *Did you examine the vehicles?*

Q: *When?*

Q: *Where?*

Q: *Did you see damage to both vehicles?*

Q: *Please describe all damage.*

Q: *Did you see any skid marks leading up to the point of impact?*

Q: *From which direction?*

Q: *Were you able to determine whether those skids had been made by one of the involved vehicles?*

Q: *How did you establish that?*

Q: *Which one?*

Q: *Did you measure those skids?*

Q: *How?*

Q: *What measurements did you obtain?*

Q: *Did you see any skidmarks leading away from the point of impact?*

Q: *Going in which direction?*

Q: *Could you tell whether those skids were caused by one of the involved vehicles?*

Q: *How?*

Q: *Which one?*

Q: *Did you measure those skids?*

Q: *How?*

Q: *What measurements did you obtain?*

Q: *Did you find any scuffs, scratches or gouges on the roadway?*

Q: *Where?*

Q: *What did those indicate to you?*

Q: *Explain.*

Q: *Did you see any damage to any objects along the paths of the vehicles?*

Q: *What?*

Q: *Where?*

Q: *Did you establish the point of rest of both vehicles?*

Q: *Where?*

Q: *Did you establish the point of rest of decedent Morton?*

Q: *Where?*

Q: *Did you observe the injuries to Morton?*

Q: *Did you notice the defendant at the scene?*

Q: *Did you see any visible injuries to him?*

Q: *Describe.*

Q: *Did you look inside both vehicles while they were at their points of rest?*

Q: *Did you see any alcoholic beverage containers in either?*

Q: *Which?*

Q: *What kind of containers?*

Q: *How many?*

Q: *Did you examine them?*

Q: *What did you find?*

Q: *Other than inside the Toyota, did you see any alcohol containers anywhere within the intersection or nearby?*

Q: *Based on the factors you previously explained, were you able to determine an estimate of the speed of the Toyota before braking?*

Q: *Please explain how you arrived at that, showing the effect of the various factors you took into consideration.*

Q: *What did you determine the speed of the Toyota to be before braking?*

Q: *On June 19, was there a posted speed on 18th Street approaching Vincent?*

Q: *Where was it posted?*

Q: *What was the posted speed?*

Q: *Were you able to determine the estimated speed of the pick-up truck prior to impact?*

Q: *Please explain how you arrived at that.*

Q: *What was the speed you established for the pick-up?*

Q: *Did you obtain statements from any persons about this accident?*

Q: *When and where?*

Q: *From whom?*

Q: *On the basis of all of the information you developed from your investigation, have you formed an opinion as to the cause of the accident?*

Q: *What is that opinion?*

Obviously, depending on the facts and issues in any given case, you may have to go into some particular thing more thoroughly, and you may not even have to mention some of these things. You would normally use lots of photographs and diagrams to help the jury understand things. And don't forget to take your pocket calculator with you (maybe a couple of toy cars, too).

I know there are a lot of other kinds of cases where you might expect to testify as an expert. But these three are probably the most common for most officers (except criminalists), and they should give you a good idea of how this qualification-and-opinion business works.

By the time most cops have been on the force for five or six years, they've forgotten some of their training and qualifications. To help you recall the things you'll be asked about, when and if you're called as an expert,

I strongly recommend, no matter what your present status and assignment, that you start right now to keep a permanent record of your training, studies and experience. Take the record with you to court. When you're asked about details that you can't recall, ask to refer to your record. I suggest a format like the following:

IN-SERVICE TRAINING				
	Date	Place	Subject	Number Hours
Basic Academy				
Advanced Academy				
Special Schools				
Roll-Call Training				

SPECIAL STUDIES/EXPERIMENTS

Dates	Place	Subject	Description

COLLEGE, UNIVERSITY, TECH SCHOOL

Dates	Place	Subject	Description

READINGS

Date	Title	Author	Description

PROFESSIONAL ASSOCIATIONS

OJT
Supervised Training

Dates	Supervisor	Subject	No. Hrs. or Cases

INVESTIGATIONS, ARRESTS, EVALUATIONS, ETC.
Approximate Number

Narc	Prints	T/A	Bookmaking	Ballistics	DWI	Handwriting	Poly

Court	Narc	Prints	T/A	Bkmkg	Ballis.	DWI	Handwriting	Poly
PRIOR EXPERT TESTIMONY **Number**								
Justice								
Municipal								
Superior								
Supreme								
Federal								
Other States								

OTHER QUALIFICATION

If you haven't been keeping this kind of record, make one up now and fill it in as best you can from memory and any records available to you. Keep the *numbers* charts in pencil, so you can update them every week (or month).

Everyone who ever becomes an expert witness has to have a "first time" to qualify. Don't be ashamed of it. You know more about your work than any of the jurors and most of the attorneys. Just approach your first few times with the confidence that you know what you're talking about, and you'll sound like an old pro sooner than you think.

□

COURTROOM
EXCELLENCE

In spite of the fact that peace officers and prosecutors are both on the law enforcement team, they don't always act like teammates toward each other. That's especially unfortunate to the extent that it hampers close coordination and works to the advantage of criminals.

Why does it sometimes go wrong? Prosecutors may get the idea that certain cops do incomplete investigations, write lousy reports, or make poor witnesses. And cops sometimes feel that certain prosecutors are too "stat-conscious," don't appreciate the problems and limitations confronting cops, and expect the cops to do too much of the prosecutor's job.

If the prosecutor thinks you did a poor job on the last case he had with you, he may be more than a little reluctant to file the next one you bring in. Or he may bargain a higher percentage of your cases because he doesn't want to try another case where you're the crucial witness. If you get into this kind of situation with a prosecutor, it doesn't take too long for it to show up in the results on your cases. Your supervisors are going to notice it, too.

I don't have any easy solutions to the cop's complaints with the prosecutor (you might ask him to ride along with you some Friday night). But it isn't too difficult to remove the prosecutor's complaints against *you:* make sure your investigations are complete and your reports are well-written before you seek a complaint, and don't give the prosecutor any cause to complain about your courtroom performance. If he knows you're going to come through for him on the witness stand, he'll be far more willing to take your cases to trial. (And remember, the *more* willing the prosecutor is to go to trial, the *less* willing the defense attorney will usually be, with the result that the crook is more likely to plead out.)

I entitled this book "COURTROOM SURVIVAL" because I wanted to get your attention. Most officers think that court *is* something they have to "survive" (or avoid). But that's only because most of them don't know what to expect, or how to handle it effectively. And that sad situation, I regret to say, is partly because those of us who have left police departments to become city attorneys, county attorneys, and district attorneys haven't always done a very good job of sharing our new insights with the departments we left.

That's especially unfortunate because there are a number of criminal justice subjects on which an officer-turned-prosecutor is exceptionally well-qualified to assist in peace officer training. Report writing is one such topic; testifying is another. But some of us have become preoccupied with our own daily prosecutorial duties, and we've left important, highly-technical training to such unlikely substitutes as English teachers and private attorneys. The only beneficiaries of this imperfect pattern are killers, robbers, rapists and other assorted crooks.

An important objective in my writing this book was to help fill the communication gap between the prosecutor and the field officer. If other prosecutors find their way through these pages, I hope they'll jump into the gap with me: it's neither fair nor intelligent for us to sit back and complain about poor reports or poor testimony if we haven't done anything to help improve them from the prosecutor's standpoint.

And if *you* should ever find yourself finishing night law school and signing on to the courthouse part of the law enforcement team, don't forget to keep sharing information with your friends at the station. There's always going to be room for one more in the gap.

"COURTROOM SURVIVAL" is the name of the book, but that's not what it's about. COURTROOM *EXCELLENCE* is the name of the game, and that's what this book is really about. It isn't enough for you to be able to get down off the stand, walk outside the courthouse, and say to yourself: "Whew! I made it through another one!" We're up against criminals who get help from legal aid, help from public defenders, help from the private defense bar, and all kinds of undeserved help from ridiculous appellate and supreme court decisions; it's just a tragic shame every time they get more help from an unprepared officer on the witness stand.

So don't just soak up enough of this book to get by. Soak up enough to **excel.** And don't be reluctant to put what you learn into practice every chance you get. If you shun the early traffic and DWI trials, you may just get your first courtroom experience in a multiple murder case. If you get a subpena for an "unimportant" case, don't dodge it—use it! Get used to being just as good on the witness stand as you are on the streets.

Then get down off the stand, walk outside the courthouse, and say to yourself: "Up against **me**, those poor dumb bastards never stood a chance!"

□

Additional books by Devallis Rutledge . . .

CRIMINAL INTERROGATION
Law and Tactics

THE NEW POLICE REPORT MANUAL

THE OFFICER SURVIVAL MANUAL

THE SEARCH and SEIZURE HANDBOOK
For Law Officers

(Order form next page)

America's Most Popular
Practical Police Books